A Prequel to the international best seller book The *Mugs & Saucers Café*

The Cabin

BEST SELLING AUTHOR
W K WAITE-GRACIE

ISBN: 978-1-964619-14-9

Thank you, sister, from another mister. You were the twinkle in this book's eye and creation.

Ab's and Gav, my beautiful WHYs, cheerleaders, and forever inspiration to just keep swimming, I love you beyond words.

And to the Me I am becoming… You are on your way to greater things Kath! Enjoy the ride, keep shining your light, and never give up on your dreams. There are many more roofs to fix yet ;)

Love and Light
Come One Sweaty Pie

Introduction

Katherine Waite-Gracie, the international best-selling author of *The Mugs & Saucers Café*, invites you to indulge in the irresistible prequel to Maggie and Billy's passionate romance. *The Cabin* delivers a week filled with love, music, unforgettable firsts, romance, newfound friendships, and sad endings. Your pulse will be racing, your smile growing, and your heart breaking as you flip through the pages of youthful lust between these two loving characters and their friends.

Table of Contents

Introduction 5

The Cabin Playlist 9

CHAPTER 1 13

CHAPTER 2 29

CHAPTER 3 42

CHAPTER 4 53

CHAPTER 5 67

CHAPTER 6 93

CHAPTER 7 116

CHAPTER 8 129

CHAPTER 9 142

CHAPTER 10 155

CHAPTER 11 167

CHAPTER 12 174

CHAPTER 13 188

About the Author 193

The Cabin Playlist

Reach Out And Touch Faith-Depeche Mode
Peggy Sue-Buddy Holly
Islands In The Stream-Kenny Rogers and Dolly Parton
Take Me Home, Country Roads-John Denver
Forever In Blue Jeans-Neil Diamond
I Love Rock'n'Roll-Joan Jett and The Blackhearts
Free Falln'-Tom Petty
Summer Of '69-Brian Adams
End Of The Line-Traveling Wilburys
Hey Jude-The Beatles
Pour Some Sugar On Me-Def Leppard
I'm On Fire- Bruce Springsteen
Angel-Aerosmith
Ain't No Sunshine-Bill Withers
Bust A Move-Young M.C.
Sweet Dreams-The Eurythmics
I Wanna Dance With Somebody-Whitney Houston
Footloose-Kenny Loggins
Rebel Yell-Billy Idol
Karma Chameleon-The Culture Club
More Than A Feeling-Boston
Fall At Your Feet-Crowded House

Sunshine-Nazareth
House Of The Rising Sun-The Animals
Girl Of Mine-Blue Rodeo
Listen To Your Heart-Roxette
Take My Breath Away-Berlin
Don't You Forget About Me-Simple Minds
Every Breath You Take-The Police
Time After Time-Cyndi Lauper
Losing My Religion-REM
Have You Ever Seen The Rain-CCR
Never Tear Us Apart-INXS
Fur Elise-Beethoven
Moonlight Sonata-Beethoven
House Of Dreams-Blue Rodeo
Into The Mystic-Van Morrison
Copperhead Road-Steve Earle
All I Want Is You-U2
Know Where You Go/Tell Me Your Dream-Blue Rodeo
Tunnel Of Love-Dire Straits
She Drives Me Crazy-Fine Young Cannibals
You Shook Me All Night Long-ACDC
Never Gonna Give You Up-Rick Astley
Don't You Want Me-The Human League
What It Takes-Aerosmith
Sweet Emotion-Aerosmith
Hungry Eyes-Eric Carmen
With Or Without You-U2

Heart Like Mine-Blue Rodeo
Let Your Love Flow-Bellamy Brothers
500 Miles-The Proclaimers
9 to 5-Dolly Parton
I Need A Hero-Bonnie Tyler
Material Girl-Madonna
It's In His Kiss-Cher
Gloria-Laura Branigan
Hit Me With Your Best Shot-Pat Benatar
Girls Just Wanna Have Fun-Cyndi Lauper
The Joker-Steve Miller Band
Jamming-Bob Marley and The Wailers
Last Dance With MaryJane-Tom Petty
Magic Carpet Ride-Steppenwolf
Red Red Wine-UB40
Head Over Heels-Tears For Fears
Bed Of Roses-Bon Jovi
More Than Words-Extreme
November Rain-Guns N'Roses
The Gambler-Kenny Rogers
Me And Bobby McGee-Janis Joplin
I Got You Babe-Sonny and Cher
Mr. Blue Sky-Electric Light Orchestra
Poison-Alice Cooper
Romeo And Juliet-Dire Straits
I Will Never Be The Same-Melissa Ethridge

CHAPTER 1

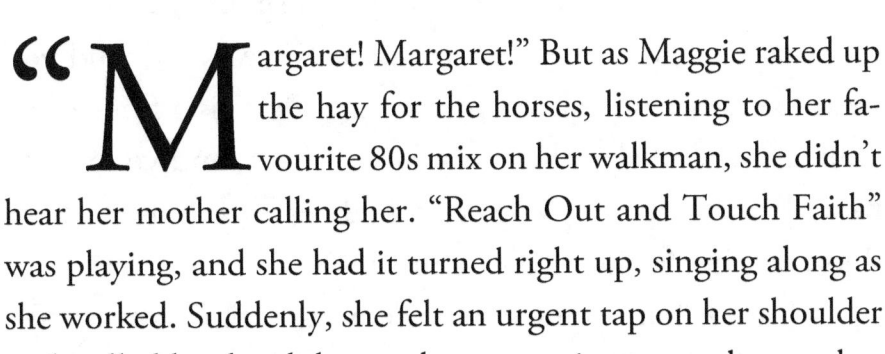

"Margaret! Margaret!" But as Maggie raked up the hay for the horses, listening to her favourite 80s mix on her walkman, she didn't hear her mother calling her. "Reach Out and Touch Faith" was playing, and she had it turned right up, singing along as she worked. Suddenly, she felt an urgent tap on her shoulder and pulled her headphones down, turning around to see her mom standing there with an irritated look on her face.

"Margaret, must you listen to that while you're doing chores!?" Maggie shrugged.

"Sorry Mom. What's up?" Her mother shook her head and gave Maggie a little grin.

"Oh Margaret, you and your music! Wish you'd spend as much time practicing your piano theory as you do listening to other people's music."

Maggie shrugged again. She loved playing the piano; it was always such a great outlet for her. She didn't enjoy the lessons and theory as much. She laughed to herself too, thinking her mom's irritation was a bit rich considering she always had music playing while she worked away in the kitchen, but Maggie decided to keep that thought to herself.

"Margaret, Peter just called. He wanted to know if he

could take you to the dance tomorrow night. I told him that would be fine." Maggie was now the one with the irritated look on her face.

"Aw, Mom. I was going to go with Bridget and Tina." Her mother shook her head slightly and spoke again.

"Margaret May Ashberry, you are 17 years old, and you need to really think about your future. Peter is a fine young man and will likely inherit his father's farm, and you would be well taken care of." Maggie scuffed her foot along the barn floor, waiting for her mom to finish.

"Mom, I don't want to be 'taken care of'! I want to take care of myself. I'm leaving for college soon, why would I want to get married?" Her mother gave her an exasperated sigh and turned to leave the barn.

"You are lucky Peter is interested in you Margaret. He'll pick you up tomorrow night at seven." And she was on her way back up to the house when she added, "I'll need your help for dinner in 10 minutes." Maggie stood there, holding the rake for a moment before walking over to her horse Benny.

"Benny, I'm turning 18 in two months, and they still expect me to listen as if I were 10. I can't wait to go to college and get off this farm!" She finished up and went inside to clean herself up before helping with dinner.

At six o'clock sharp, her dad and brothers filed into the kitchen.

"Mmm, smells good Ma!" Mason, her oldest of three brothers, said as he passed their mom.

"Wash up boys, it's ready," she said smiling. Her mom turned down the oldies radio station she loved and you could just barely hear "Peggy Sue" playing. Her dad went over to the sink and washed his hands, scrubbing right up to his elbows. Maggie's mom passed him a towel with a smile. He dried up, and while handing it back to her pulled her close and kissed her. Then he headed for his spot at the table and sat down.

"Hi Dad," Maggie said as he passed her, giving him a kiss on the cheek.

"Hello Margaret, I hear you have a special night planned for tomorrow?" he said, smiling at her as he sat in his chair at the head of the table. Her mother brought over a bowl of homemade chicken soup and set it down in front of him. "Thanks, dear," he said, and she gave him a little kiss on the cheek. Maggie watched as he reached up and gently rubbed her arm as she walked away. Most people thought it was gross when their parents were affectionate, but Maggie had always loved how much her parents seemed to care about each other. She'd never known another man as loving and faithful as her dad. Of course, the guys in school weren't married, but they were certainly not faithful. She had an uncle who'd cheated on her aunt, her father's older sister, leaving her so devastated she died of a broken heart. Maggie thought that must be one of the worst endings to life. There was always talk around town of quite a few couples with roaming husbands too. Maggie didn't like the idea that fooling around was such a common practice, which might have been an additional factor in why she loved how much her parents loved one another, even in hard times. She often watched with a warm smile as they enjoyed their rare moments alone together, walking hand in hand around the farm or dancing together in the kitchen.

Her father started eating his soup. He had quite an appetite as a farmer whose work began at five in the morning and ended at 6 every night. He was such a hard worker and always so busy with the farm. Maggie's mom motioned to her to come and grab the platters and bowls that held dinner and start placing them on the table.

"Yes, Dad, I'm going to the end-of-summer dance tomorrow." He looked up and smiled.

"Yes, your mother tells me that nice young man Peter Baker is taking you?" She was so annoyed but held her tongue and nodded. Her dad went back to eating his soup which was now almost gone.

Just then, Mason, Fred, and Frankie came back in, taking their spots at the table and jumping right in to eat. Maggie and her mom sat down and joined them. The guys and her dad talked about how they needed to fix the tractor, what parts they needed, and how it would soon be haying time again. Her dad mentioned that their old cow, Edith, was getting on and they discussed options, trying to figure out what to do with her. Mason talked about how excited he was to be going off to Cadet's School soon. Maggie sat quietly, eating her dinner, and thinking about what she might wear to the dance. Her brother Frankie sat across from her. He was the baby of the family and her favourite. Still only nine, he was a goofball and was making faces at her from across the table. She giggled and felt an inward appreciation for his kind, silly, lighthearted nature. He was more like Maggie than the other two. He and Maggie spent a lot of time together. Frankie liked the same things as Maggie and she was a fun big sister. They spent many free hours having dance parties in Maggie's room, rocking out to their favourite tunes, talking about the boys Maggie liked in school, watching old movies together, or looking through magazines and pointing out which fashions they preferred. They also did most of their chores together unless Frankie was needed to help with the 'manly' stuff. Although Maggie basically did all the same work, used just as much energy and muscle power, knew how to run all the equipment and take care of the animals, and spent just as much time farming as her brothers did, she was still seen as 'the girl,' and when she wasn't out doing chores, she was inside helping her mom do the *woman's* work'.

After she and her mom cleaned up the dinner dishes, Maggie grabbed her current favourite book, Anne of Green Gables, and went back outside. She made her way to the stables, and approached Benny, her black horse. "Hello Benny," she said to him with a smile. He gave a happy little snort in response and whinnied as Maggie reached up and stroked his face. "Feel like a walk old friend?" she asked, opening his stall and walking him out. She didn't bother grabbing the saddle. She wouldn't be doing any hard riding as he was getting older, and their walks were more out of companionship and habit. She climbed up with ease, gently tangling her fingers in his dark mane. Then they walked the long way to the path through the woods behind their house and found Maggie's favourite tree to sit under. She left him nearby in the long grass so he could graze while she sat at the bottom of the tree to read.

A few of the barn cats soon joined her and their dog Buddy eventually sniffed her out and laid down beside her too. She loved this spot, hidden away under the canopy of leaves, sitting at the roots of her favourite willow tree, surrounded by animals and nature. She could just see through the trees enough to watch the glow of the sun setting beyond the woods if she managed to get there in time. That was where she spent most of her evenings if she wasn't riding or out with her friends. Usually surrounded by animals and often with her nose stuck in a book. She was finding it hard to focus on her reading though and found herself lost in thought, looking forward to the dance tomorrow. She would much rather go with her friends, but they would still be there, and she could hang out with them once she and Pete arrived.

She'd known Pete all her life. His family had a farm about a mile from *her* family's farm. It was just him, his brother, and their dad. It had been just the three of them for most of Pete's life. His mom had died when he was very young and being the oldest, he became his fathers right-hand man. He was a year older than Maggie and he was very cute and charming, and a lot of girls liked him. Actually, *he* liked a lot of girls. Growing up together and living so close, they had spent a lot of time hanging out, helping each other's families on their farms, and they got along pretty well. Although Pete was perhaps a bit too cocky at times, he was nice enough, though she really didn't like being pushed into dating him. She also didn't like how much time he spent with so many different girls. He had been 'after' her for a few years now and had been spending more and more time over at their farm, chatting with her brothers and helping her dad. Maggie knew he was just working on getting closer to her, and she should be flattered, but she wasn't. *Oh well, what will it hurt, getting a ride with Pete?* she thought as she sat in the last light of the setting sun, patting Buddy.

The next evening, she finished up her chores early and was excused from dinner duty to get ready for the dance. She put on her favourite green dress with the little daisies embroidered on the skirt, black flats, and grabbed her black sweater. Her long golden brown curls fell down her back as she applied just a little bit of peach-coloured lipstick. She was just finishing up putting in her daisy earrings, spritzing on her favourite vanilla perfume, and staring into her own emerald eyes in the reflection of her mirror when she heard her mother calling from the kitchen.

"Margaret, Peter's here." She couldn't help feeling a bit

excited about her date and proceeded down to the kitchen with her usual, big Maggie smile.

"Hello Pete," she said as she entered the room. Her parents were both smiling at the two of them.

"Hello, Maggie. You look nice," he told her, grinning and holding his arm up for her to link hers through. He nodded at her parents and said, "Mr. and Mrs. Ashberry." and escorted her out.

"Bye Mom, bye Dad!" she called back as they left.

"You kids have fun," she heard her mother say as she closed the door behind them.

Peter opened the truck door for her and she climbed in. As soon as he got in and started the truck up, he looked over at her, smiling broadly.

"Maggie, you look good enough to eat," he told her. She wasn't sure she liked that thought but smiled just the same. Off they went into town, pulling up to the arena and parking at the end of a long row of other vehicles. "Wow, looks like a lot of people are here tonight," Pete said as he turned the truck off and hopped out. Maggie climbed out and closed her door, joining him. Before going any further, Pete stopped her, holding one of her hands. "You know Maggie, I've been wanting to take you out for a long time." He grabbed her butt and pulled her close, leaning down to kiss her. She turned her head slightly just before he planted one on her and he kissed her cheek instead.

"Yes, I know Pete, but let's see how tonight goes before

we move too fast. No reason to start getting too grabby." She smiled and walked towards the front doors. The lights were still on when they went inside, the music playing quietly as more and more people were arriving. She saw Bridget and Tina over at a table near the back, waving at her. "Just going to go freshen up, Pete," she said and motioned to her friends to follow her. The three of them went into the bathroom and started chattering.

"Ohhh, you look so pretty tonight Maggie!" Tina said.

"You're so lucky, coming here with Peter Baker!" Bridget added. Maggie smiled but inwardly thought, *Ya, he's alright, but he's not my Prince Charming.* They chatted and giggled a little more then went back to a table together where Pete and two of his friends joined them. The lights had started to dim, and the music was getting louder. These town dances usually played mostly country and oldies music, which Maggie enjoyed as she just loved all music in general. "Islands in the Stream" was playing and Maggie wanted to dance.

"Come on Pete, let's dance!" she smiled at him eagerly.

"Nah, let's wait for a slow song, eh Maggie?" Her shoulders dropped a little, but her two friends were game, so the three of them went out to the dance floor together, singing and dancing and laughing with each other. After dancing to a couple more songs, they went back to the guys at the table and sat down. They had gotten the girls some drinks. "Got you a screwdriver Maggie," Pete said as she picked it up and smelled it.

"Oh, thanks, Pete. Actually, I'd rather just have a pop though." He looked thoroughly disappointed.

"Come on Maggie, live a little!" He and the other guys held their glasses up. She just looked at him with an unimpressed stare.

"Ok, ok, Maggie, I won't get you another one, but how about just drinking this one, seeing as I already paid for it, then I'll get you pop the rest of the night?" She decided that was fine and drank it quickly so she could get it over with. She really wasn't a fan of alcohol - the taste or the effects - but figured one wouldn't hurt. After that, the girls danced on their own for ages, then they decided to get the guys up dancing too. It took a little persuading, but finally, a slow song came on and Pete agreed. He pulled Maggie tightly against him as they danced. She was having fun, and Pete was always a little nicer when his friends weren't listening. They ended up having a good time, and around 12:30, Maggie asked Pete to take her home.

"Bye Maggie!" her friends yelled as she and Pete left the arena together. Before turning down the road to Maggie's, Pete pulled off to the side and turned down a driveway at an old, abandoned farmhouse, then shut the engine off.

"What's up Pete?" she asked, thinking there was something wrong with the truck. He left the interior light on and turned to look at her with an almost devious stare.

"You look *really* good tonight Maggie," he told her. She smiled.

"Thanks, Pete." He really was very cute, and she did feel some attraction towards him. She knew what he was hoping for but just couldn't shake the fact that he'd been with so many girls already. Maybe it wouldn't have bugged her so much if she hadn't been friends with so many of them. He moved closer, putting his arm around her and leaning in for a kiss. This time she didn't turn her head. She closed her eyes and felt his lips touch hers. Her stomach gave a little flip, feeling his lips pressing against hers. The kiss was nice. *A little slobbery*, she thought to herself, maybe because of the drinks he'd had and his eagerness to 'have' Maggie. He was definitely well-practiced and seemed to like skipping ahead to last base. He was sticking his tongue down her throat and feeling her up within the first 30 seconds of the kiss. Things were escalating and quickly heating up, especially for Pete. After a few minutes of more intense kisses and groping, his hands started to move to the back of her dress, fumbling to undo her bra, and Maggie pulled back and moved his hands.

"Whoa, Pete. Let's slow down a bit." He leaned down to kiss her again. They kissed some more and then he tried to undress her again. "Pete, really, slow down." He sat up straight, slid back over in front of the steering wheel, and started the truck up.

"Okay, Maggie. But I won't wait for you forever," he said and drove her home.

After a goodnight kiss, Maggie opened her door.

"Thanks for the ride, Pete," she said as she hopped out

and closed the door. Walking into the house and up the stairs towards her room, she opened her door and entered. Maggie was thinking about how much fun she had dancing the night away, then thinking about Pete. There really wasn't anyone else from school or town that she'd want to be with. She'd actually been hoping and dreaming she'd meet someone when she went away to college, and he'd whisk her away from her farm life. She did like Pete well enough and thought he'd probably make a decent enough boyfriend or husband one day, but her gut was trying to tell her something. She wasn't sure if it was that he wasn't the one, or that she was just nervous about having a serious boyfriend. *Maybe I am going too slow*, she thought to herself. Am I being too picky? *I mean, Pete and I have been hanging out for years together, he's been pursuing me for a while now... I am 17 and haven't even gone all the way with anyone yet. Maybe I should do it with Pete.* She got undressed and changed into her pajamas, used the washroom, and was heading back to her room when she heard Frankie's door open. He peeked his face out to see who was up.

"Hey sis," he whispered, and she grinned at him. He came out of his room and closed the door quietly behind him, coming over to her. He stood there, looking at her expectantly. Maggie grinned at him and held her door open and the two of them went inside. Frankie sat at the end of her bed and grinned. "Soooo, how was your date?" She knew he was teasing, but she laughed anyway.

"Now, that's none of your business little brother," she replied, giving him a wink.

"Oh, come on, was Peter Baker a gentleman Magster?" he giggled and she threw a pillow at him as she sat down at the head of her bed. He picked it up and threw it back.

"No, not really!" she answered him, rolling her eyes and giggling. "But I was!" she added, smiling. He shook his head at her and laughed.

"Peter and Maggie, sitting in a tree," he started to chant, Maggie threw the pillow at him again. Frankie ducked and giggled.

"You better get to bed Frankie before you get busted." He stuck his tongue out at her and jumped off her bed. Then he pretended to dance around making kissing noises and singing "Peter and Maggie," again. Maggie laughed and ruffled his hair playfully, walking him to her door.

"Night sis," he said, leaving her room.

The summer days all melded together for Maggie. Up at five, milking at five-thirty, feeding the animals, shoveling out the muck, helping with meals, evening rides on Benny, and sunsets in the woods under her tree. Except for some random visits from Bridget and Tina and her and Pete spending more time together now that they were officially dating, she was pretty much chained to the farm.

One night, at the end of October, Pete came by the farm and surprised her with flowers and asked her parents if they'd mind if he took her out for the night. It was Maggie's birthday, and she and her family were still sitting around the kitchen table together. Her parents and her brothers had already given her their gifts and had all enjoyed their pieces of chocolate cheesecake. Frankie made her a bracelet with pretty glass beads that he'd been collecting for quite some time using all her favourite colours. Fred and Mason went in on a Blue Rodeo cassette tape for her, and her parents gave her a beautiful, silver heart-shaped locket on a chain that Maggie was already wearing.

"Would you like some cake, Peter?" Mrs. Ashberry asked, ready to cut him a piece.

"Oh, thank you, but no. I'm just fine Mrs. Ashberry," he said very politely.

She smiled at him, then she said, "Okay Peter, well, it's nice you want to take Margaret out. That sounds lovely, doesn't it Margaret?" she said, smiling over at her. Maggie smiled automatically, knowing her parents were more than happy to say yes to Peter's request to take Maggie out (whether Maggie was feeling like going out or not). Maggie got up and took her dishes to the sink. Then, Maggie thanked everyone for her gifts, and for a great dinner, grabbed her sweater, and headed out with Pete. They drove down to the pond on the other side of town and Pete parked the truck and hopped out. She heard him doing something in the back and then heard him close the tailgate, still managing to get to Maggie's side before she had climbed out and opened the door for her, taking her hand to help her down.

She was a little surprised at his charm as there wasn't even an audience. He didn't seem to be carrying anything but had a funny, nervous look on his face as he took her hand and led her down to a grassy spot under a tree. The water was completely calm, and the evening air was still quite warm. She was looking out over the water when she felt his hand on her arm and turned to see him kneeling beside her with a little pink box opened up in his hand.

"Happy birthday Maggie!" he said to her, smiling. "Maggie, I have wanted you for a long time now, and I would be honoured if you would marry me." she stared at him in disbelief for a moment. "Maggie?" he said.

"Oh, sorry Pete." She looked down at the box and saw a gold band with a sweet little diamond in the middle. "Umm, well thank you, Pete, can I think about it?" was all she could say. He looked a little surprised but nodded at her.

"Ah, sure. But not for too long I hope." He gave her a little smile.

"Right," she answered. The rest of the evening was fairly quiet. Of course, there was a bit of a make-out session, but she never let things go too far. He ended up taking her home once the sun had set.

They continued to date, and she continued to avoid giving him a definite answer to his proposal, always finding an excuse to prolong things. Their make-out sessions became increasingly heated as they managed to cover most of the bases. Maggie still didn't want to go all the way with him, though. She still felt a bit weird about all the girls he'd already slept with and didn't want to be just another girl conquered on his list. She felt like there was something else out there waiting for her. New adventures she didn't want to be tied down for.

CHAPTER 2

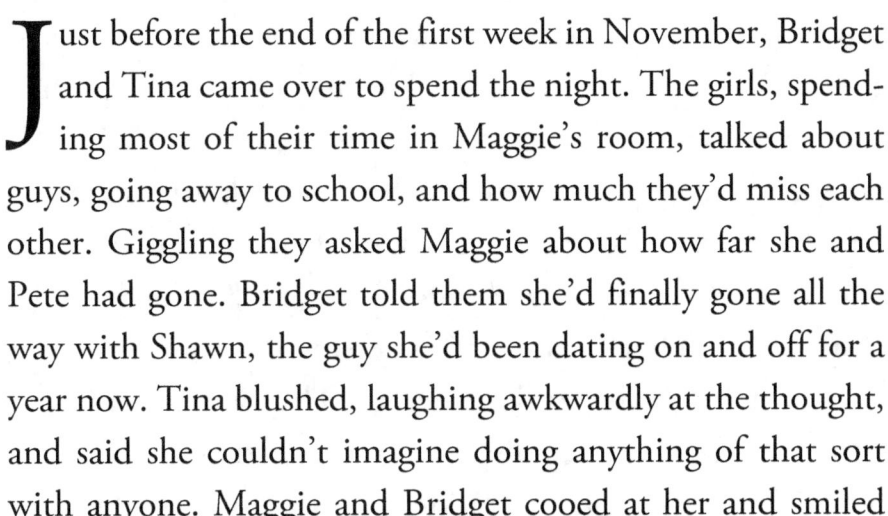

J ust before the end of the first week in November, Bridget and Tina came over to spend the night. The girls, spending most of their time in Maggie's room, talked about guys, going away to school, and how much they'd miss each other. Giggling they asked Maggie about how far she and Pete had gone. Bridget told them she'd finally gone all the way with Shawn, the guy she'd been dating on and off for a year now. Tina blushed, laughing awkwardly at the thought, and said she couldn't imagine doing anything of that sort with anyone. Maggie and Bridget cooed at her and smiled affectionately at her embarrassment. They talked about their dreams and plans and what they wished they could do, but until they were away from home, they had to keep following their parents' boring rules.

Bridget told Maggie and Tina about how her older sister had gone away to this cabin in the mountains for her 21st birthday. She rented it for a couple of weeks with a large group of friends. They went skiing and snowboarding, and the cabin had been completely free of parents. The only people there were the groups who rented it. Bridget talked about how much she wanted to do the same trip, and that the more people who went, the better. She thought they should do it before everyone went away to school. Maggie had plans to go away to nursing college, but in the end, applied to a nearby school as her parents said she was still needed on the farm. It hadn't been her dream, but she'd still be able to take her courses during the evenings and be able to help her parents during the day. She could do some of her placement hours and then work part time at their local doctor's office after graduation. Her brother Mason would be leaving for the Air Cadets, and her family needed her to stay home to help run things.

"That sounds like so much fun Bridget!" Maggie said, excitedly, dreaming of the freedom. And so, with that, the plans began. They'd have to fly there, which was something none of them had ever done before. They would arrive the first Saturday in December, and stay until the following weekend, on Sunday. She, Bridget, Tina, and one other girl, Cindy, from their old school clique, got to work on all the planning, making arrangements, getting their tickets, and packing and repacking what they'd bring. Cindy was bringing her boyfriend Dave and his friends Sam and Chris had decided to come too. Pete wasn't going to be able to come, because his brother was away at school, and his dad couldn't run the farm on his own. Maggie didn't mind, though. Although she and Pete had been dating since the summer dance, and it had been a number of weeks since he proposed, she still hadn't given him an answer and she was actually looking forward to getting away and enjoying some freedom before having to settle down, still undecided on whether or not that's what she was going to end up doing.

Her parents weren't too happy about her leaving, well more so, her dad. "You're needed here Margaret, and a young lady shouldn't be going off to a strange place without chaperones. And what about church, Margaret? Missing two Sundays in a row!" Had been what he said one night when she was gathering up her belongings. They hadn't said no, but she was feeling guilty about leaving and grumpy that they were making her feel bad.

Her mom took her aside one day and said, "Margaret, your father and I will find a way to get things sorted while you are gone. I don't want you to worry about anything, okay? You know your dad will come around. He's just got to be Papa Bear with his only daughter. Enjoy yourself, Margaret; it might be your last getaway before settling down with Peter." She was surprised that her mom knew. But when she opened her mouth to say something, her mom stopped her. "Moms always know Margaret. Just promise me you'll have fun." Maggie nodded at her and gave her mom a hug.

As November came to an end and became colder and wetter, they were becoming more and more eager for a change of scenery and their adventure away. Their plans were all set for them to go. Every chance the friends had to hang out, the trip was all they could talk about. They were all so excited, and Maggie was finding it hard not to talk about it too much around Pete. He was not at all happy she was going without him.

"I'm sorry you can't come Pete. Maybe we can do the trip again when your brother is back home," she said to him one afternoon only a few days before she would be leaving. She was out in the barn with him on his farm, helping him with chores, and he was trying to get her to change her mind.

"Maggie, I don't want you to go. What am I gonna do while you're gone for a whole week? I don't think you should go away with a bunch of guys when we're engaged." She stopped what she was doing and glared at him.

"Peter Baker, we are not even officially engaged. I never said yes." He opened his mouth to speak again, but she cut him off. "Annnd, I am not going away with a bunch of guys. Some guys are coming with us girls, that have nothing to do with me, and you don't get to tell me what I can and can't do!" He looked at her for a second, a look of surprise on his face then threw down the rake he was holding into the pile of hay next to him and walked toward her. He had taken his shirt off while they had been busily working and his skin was shiny with sweat, making the muscles in his arms more pronounced, and the look of determination on his face was quite intense. He stopped right in front of her and just stared. He actually looked quite attractive, at that moment. She found that after all their years together, she did feel a fondness for him and was feeling more and more like she might even consider giving herself to him. *Not like movie love though,* she thought to herself.

As he headed for her, she wasn't sure what he was going

to do. She had never really stood up for herself like that before. Maggie had her hands on her hips and stood her ground, looking back with just as much determination. Then, all of a sudden, he grabbed her, his arms wrapped around her waist, and he picked her up. The two of them fell into the pile of hay, laughing. Then he was kissing her hard, and the suddenness of his reaction made her heart race. She kissed him back, her arms around him and holding onto his shoulders as they rolled about in the hay. She found it all very enjoyable, and when he started taking her clothes off, she didn't stop him, rubbing his back and letting him grab her ass and feel her up. When he tried to undo her pants, she snapped out of their raging hormonal fog and sat up.

"What are you doing Maggie?" he asked, suddenly irritated again.

"I don't think we should do this here or before we're married Pete," she answered as she found her bra and pulled it back on.

"Just thought, you know, before you go away, we'd, you know?!" Maggie gaped at him, then laughed and shook her head.

"I think we should wait, Pete." He flopped over with an irritated sigh.

"God, Maggie, we're as good as married! And what's the big deal? You're on the pill now, right?" he asked with a serious expression on his face. Maggie laughed again.

"That docsn't mean we should jump right into sex Pete!"

She told him, grabbing her shirt. He hit the ground beside him with his fist in frustration.

"I'm gonna get going Pete. I still have to finish my own chores at home," Maggie told him, and after doing her bra back up, she pulled her shirt on and grabbed her jacket, and ran off.

Pete was pretty cold the next day, but by the night before the gang left, he had warmed up again and regained his usual cocky arrogance. He came by her place at dinner, and while her family was all sitting around the table, announced his proposal. They were all so pleased and didn't even ask if she'd said yes. She was pissed, and when they were alone again, told him so.

"Pete, why did you tell my family that? I haven't even said yes yet!" He grinned cockily at her.

"You'll say yes Maggie. After you get back from your trip, you'll say yes, and then we'll be able to plan officially." She didn't bother arguing with him. It wasn't worth it. He kissed her goodnight and goodbye, and she spent the next hour sitting on the bench out in front of the farm, daydreaming about her week away. Little did she know in that moment how much that week would affect the rest of her life.

The next morning, bright and early, Bridget's dad pulled up in their four-door pickup. The girls were all inside the cab, and the three guys and all the luggage were in the back bed of the truck. Off they went, Maggie waving at her family happily. She was so excited about getting away. It was about an hour's drive to the airport and time flew by as the girls chatted excitedly about their adventure. When they arrived at the drop-off area, the seven friends climbed out of the truck, gathered up their things, and thanked Bridget's dad for the ride. Bridget said goodbye and joined the group, and they found their way to their terminal and then to their seats on the plane.

"Oh my goodness, this is so cool," Tina said as the three friends filed into their row of seats.

"Did you see Pete this morning, Maggie?" Bridget asked.

"No, we said goodbye last night," she answered.

Both Tina and Bridget said "Oooooh!" grinning at her.

"What?" Maggie asked, then seeing the looks on their faces added, "Oh, no, nothing like that. He's still pissed that I'm going." Their smiles disappeared. One of the guys came over and landed right across the three of them in their laps.

"Sam! Get off!" they laughed, trying to push him up. He didn't budge.

"You ladies ready for a wicked week with the Samster?" he asked them, grinning.

"Oh Sam, get off!!!" they said again, and he stood up, soon to be ushered back to his seat by the flight attendant as the girls giggled in his direction. Then they heard the pilot tell them to buckle up, announcing they would be taking off momentarily, and the three friends squealed excitedly. It was a short flight, barely giving them a chance to dream up all the possibilities awaiting them or to imagine the people they would meet. All they knew was that it was going to be their gang and one other group of friends around their age staying in the cabin for the week, and they hoped the other group would be fun to hang out with.

When they landed, they were quick to get off the plane and grab their luggage, too excited to waste any of their highly anticipated potential fun time. They hailed a cab in front of the airport, and Bridget gave the driver the address her sister had written down for her when they first started their epic plans. An hour later, after driving deeper into the woods and higher into the mountains, they drove up a long driveway and into an open, snowy space. In a clearing, nestled in a wide surrounding of snow-covered mountains, going on for miles circling all around them with the sun just starting to set, was the cabin. Smoke was billowing from the chimney, a warm glow of golden light coming from the front windows and a string of multi-coloured Christmas lights, along the porch roof shimmered in the soft, misty snow that had started to fall.

"Ohh, it's so beautiful!" Maggie said as the taxi pulled up in front of the cabin. They paid him, grabbed their things, and went inside.

Maggie was in awe of the beauty and just stood there, soaking it up, following her friends inside. The downstairs was completely open with walls made of full-length logs, something she'd never seen before. There was a pool table, a jukebox, a pinball machine, a piano, and a TV on the opposite side of the couches, as well as a couple of easy chairs, and a fireplace. There was a large open space in the center, and at the back was the kitchen with an island acting as the barrier wall with about 20 bar stools lined up beside each other along the living room side of the island counter. There was a wide sliding glass door on the back wall of the kitchen as well, but Maggie couldn't see what was out there with the bright, setting sun shining in through the glass. Next to the kitchen was a huge, wide log staircase that went up to an open balcony-type landing, and she could see a number of doors up there. It was just so beautiful. There were eight other people there already. A couple was sitting on the bar stools, another couple lingered in the kitchen, making something together, and what looked to be two more couples were sitting on the couches in front of a roaring fire.

Just then she heard Sam call out, "Hey fellow Cabiners!" Maggie looked over to see him approaching the group at the fireplace. Scanning the couch, she saw the guy on the end who had just waved at Sam, and not too far from him on the same couch was a brunette who looked like she might be asleep. On the other couch, another guy was sitting with a guitar in his lap, strumming quietly, and there was a pretty blonde sitting closely beside him. Maggie's eyes lingered on the guitar guy, he was very cute, and he looked up at her, smiled, and then winked at her. She felt her legs give out a little and a full-body tingle ran through her as she smiled back, rather self-consciously. The guy that waved at Sam got up and walked towards them.

"Hey cabin mates, I'm Jon." Everyone smiled and said hello. He had dirty blond hair running straight down his back, all the way to his waist. He wore a tie-dye T-shirt and looked like he'd been at the bong all day. "Let me show you to your rooms, dudes." With a chuckle added, "And dudettes." They all grinned at each other, picked up their things, and followed. When they got to the top of the stairs, they saw that 12 doors were running along the back wall, and at the end of each were two more doors with a men's and women's sign on each of them.

"Kay, the last eight rooms are free to take," he chuckled. "Well, not the locked ones of course, and the washrooms are at either end." He pointed them out. "Catch you later!" he said before he went back downstairs. Cindy and Dave tried the first door, but it seemed to be one of the locked ones, so they took the next room. The two single guys skipped the next door as it was locked as well, taking the one next to it, and Maggie, Bridget, and Tina took the last room, room 12, at the end, nearest to the bathrooms. Grinning from ear to ear, Maggie and her friends went into their room. It wasn't very big, but it had large bunk beds on either side of the room that looked quite comfortable with dressers at the ends of both. The window on the back wall was huge and was actually a sliding glass door that opened onto a small 4x4 foot balcony, and they had an amazing view of the mountains and the sun setting.

"Wow! This place is beautiful!" Tina said with wonder in her eyes. They each picked their bunks, Maggie took one of the top ones, and then they used the washrooms. Once again, they were awestruck. Complete with the usual; toilets, showers, and a changing room, there was also a sauna in the corner.

"This place totally kicks butt!" yelled Bridget as they went back out onto the landing and looked down into the common area. They could see that Sam and Chris were already down there sitting on the couch with Jon and the sleeping girl. The place *was* amazing, and Maggie was so glad she hadn't let Pete talk her out of coming. Cindy and Dave's room already had a scarf tied to the doorknob and the three girls giggled as they walked past and went downstairs. The couples in the kitchen waved and said hello as the girls walked past and joined the group in the living room. Bridget and Tina sat on the couch with Guitar Guy and Pretty Blonde, as Maggie was calling them in her head, and Maggie sat in one of the big easy chairs across from where Tina was sitting on the end of the couch. Sam was first to speak up, as usual, he was Mr. Outgoing. He pointed at himself, Chris, Bridget, Tina, and Maggie saying each of their names as he did so, then he pointed at the other cabin visitors and they each said their names. Jon, whom they had met, the sleeping girl's name was Gwen, and then there was Billy, AKA Cute Guitar Guy, and Tammy, AKA Pretty Blonde. As Billy said his name, he looked straight at Maggie and their eyes locked for a moment. Again, Maggie felt electricity tingling from her head to her toes, and feeling herself blushing, she looked back at Bridget as she heard her speak.

"So when did you all get here?" asked Bridget, looking around.

"Oh, we got here yesterday morning," answered Jon in his surfer way. "Say, anybody hungry?" Jon asked the newcomers. They were, so he took them into the kitchen and explained that there was *some* food, and they could help themselves, but they were all planning on renting one of the cabin buses the next day and going into town to do some shopping for the week. "Oh, hey, there's beer in the fridge, think there's some vodka and rum left, and maybe still some pop, and if you want to join me on the balcony in room 3, we can go for a trip together," he chuckled, his soon to become known as The Jon Chuckle, over their week together.

After they introduced themselves to the two couples in the kitchen, Becky and Justin and Kim and Adam, they had a bite to eat and made some drinks. Soon, they had the music playing on the jukebox. A few people started to play pool and Jon, Gwen, Chris, and Sam disappeared. They didn't see Cindy and Dave until much later, and when they came down, they had red faces, were quite hungry, and were still all over each other. Kim and Adam were playing pinball together, and shortly after Cindy and Dave had returned, Sam, Chris, Gwen, and Jon came down looking pretty shiny and happy (as well as thirsty and hungry) and finished off the last of the snacks quickly. It was probably after one when Maggie noticed the couples in both groups had gone to bed leaving Chris, Sam, Bridget, Tina, Jon, Gwen, and herself lounging on the couches. Sam and Jon were fast friends and talking away, Gwen was stoned and passed out again on the end of the couch.

"So, are you and Gwen an item?" Sam asked Jon.

"Gwen and me? Nah, just friends, man. Only couples with us are Becky and Justin, who've been together forever, and Kim and Adam just hooked up before we came here. Why man, looking for some love'n?" he chuckled.

"Wouldn't say no to some love'n," Sam answered, and he laughed harder than he would have if he hadn't been stoned.

"Well, there's always Tammy man. She's pretty open in the love department, and don't know the story on your dudettes, but you never know, there could be some possibilities there man." They high-fived, grinning at Maggie, Bridget, and Tina. Tina's face went red, and Maggie and Bridget rolled their eyes and shook their heads at them. "Hey, well, maybe you're not interested in the ladies. You could always try Billy," Jon added, chuckling again. "As far as I know he likes the ladies, but he doesn't seem to be interested much in Tammy, and she's been trying to hook up with him since we got here. Weird too, cuz she's a real looker man, seems awfully eager too, so one never knows dude!" Maggie and Bridget rolled their eyes again and laughed. Shortly after that, the three friends went up to bed. They chatted away for quite some time, talking about what they thought of the cabin and the new people they had just met.

CHAPTER 3

The next day started late for most of the guests. Maggie woke up fairly early, and she laid in bed for a while, hoping Bridget and Tina would wake up soon too. When they didn't, she decided to go down on her own and was very thankful to find there was already coffee made, so she helped herself to a full mug and sat on the couch to enjoy it. Becky and Justin were sitting in front of a small fire, snuggled up together on the other couch.

"Morning," they said as she sat down.

"Morning," she replied with a smile.

"Where's your group?" Becky asked her.

"Oh, all still sleeping, I suppose. I'm a bit of an early riser myself." They smiled at her.

"Ya, us too. We got up and watched the sunrise. Gorgeous from this location!" Justin said with a smile.

"Oh, I bet," replied Maggie thinking she'd make sure to enjoy that at least once during one of her mornings there. "So, are people really going into town today to shop?" she asked them, enjoying another sip of her coffee.

"Oh yes, we called for the bus about half an hour ago," Becky answered. "Should be here soon, they told us." Maggie nodded. They sat quietly, drinking their coffees, and watching as people slowly made their way downstairs and joined them. By about 11 am, everyone was up. Well, Cindy and Dave were up and then back in their room with the scarf back on the doorknob after their breakfast. The bus had been dropped off, and half of them were getting ready to go. Maggie and Bridget joined Becky, Justin, Sam, Jon, Billy, Chris, and Tammy on the bus. Tina had stayed behind, not feeling up to bouncing around in the bus after a night with her first binge of alcohol, vowing "never to drink again." Gwen was staying behind, heading back to bed for a nap, and Cindy and Dave were, well, *busy*.

Bridget sat in a seat near the back and found Jon sitting down next to her before Maggie got on the bus. So, Maggie went to the seat behind them, in front of the one Tammy was sitting in, and was soon joined by Cute Guitar Guy. He stopped beside the seat and smiled at her.

"Mind if I join you?" he asked, and she shook her head and smiled a big Maggie smile back.

"Be my guest," she answered, staring at him dreamily. They smiled at each other, and Maggie felt her cheeks getting warmer before peeling her eyes away from his beautiful face and looking out the window. Still grinning as she stared out at the mountains and snow, she was instantly fantasizing about what was under his clothes. Imagining how strong his body was. Thinking about what his skin smelled like and finding herself shuddering at the thought of his warmth next to her. Feeling her cheeks going quite red, she tried to bring herself back down to Earth so she could face him again without looking too silly and googly-eyed.

It was about 10 minutes into town and the drive was absolutely breathtaking. The road down from the mountains wound in a big S shape through tall, dense forest and past a frozen lake. Adam was their designated bus driver, and Kim was sitting up in the seat right behind him. He was playing the only cassette tape that came with the bus and singing along to John Denver songs. They were all sitting together, getting to know one another, talking about what everyone had planned for the week. Maggie and Cute Guitar Guy ended up hitting it off and chatted all the way into town. She was now calling him Billy rather than Cute Guitar Guy. Although she still thought about it every time she looked at him.

Once they arrived, they all split up into a few smaller groups, each group with their own lists and pooled and divided money. Maggie and Bridget were on fruit and veggie duty and made their way to the little market, happily walking up the narrow, slanting streets with views of the mountains all around them. There were cute little clothing shops that had funky and brightly coloured designed storefronts, a few ski and snowboard places that rented out to visitors, a small skiing chalet at the top of the hill, what looked like a drug store, a market grocery store, a coffee shop, beer and liquor store, a fish and chips restaurant, and a pizza parlor. All of the shops were painted pretty colours and the whole street had a quaint feel to it with outstanding surroundings and beautiful views. Maggie and Bridget bought all the produce on their list, and Bridget even got flirty with the bag boy when they cashed out. The two girls had a good giggle about what Bridget would like to do with that bag boy if she got the chance. They all met back at the bus after half an hour with lots of food, lots of coffee, and lots of alcohol. On the way back they decided to drop the food off and head back out for a few hours of skiing. Maggie wasn't going to go as she had never skied before, but Bridget really wanted to go. Billy overheard them and when Bridget went up to get her snowsuit, he sat down next to Maggie.

"I could teach you how to ski if you like?" His eyes smiled as he looked at her. She felt so dizzy and giddy around him. Her heart raced at the mere thought of him.

"Oh really? I don't know if I'm teachable," she answered with a smile but had already decided she'd go with them and just stay in the chalet while the others skied. So as the others rented their skis and snowboards and made their way to the slopes, Maggie found a nice, cozy corner with a lovely view of the skiers and watched happily.

"Sure you won't join us?" She turned and saw Billy standing there in his gear, holding his skis and grinning at her hopefully. Smiling back, holding herself in the chair so she didn't jump right into his arms, she shook her head slightly.

"No, best not. I have a feeling I might just end up rolling down the hill," she answered. Billy was quiet for a moment, his cheeks flushing slightly, seemingly holding back. Then he replied.

"Might not be so bad if you had someone to roll down the hill with you." His eyes twinkled mischievously. Her heart was in her throat, staring at him with a goofy grin on her face. Their eyes locked for a few seconds, and Maggie felt like she could see into her future, her whole body filling with warmth. Billy reached out and touched her shoulder as he walked away. The electricity between them was palpable as he touched her.

"See you later," he said, and she waited a second before turning and watching him strut towards the door. Maggie turned around and sat back in her chair, almost giggling out loud with bubbling emotion. She made sure to make a note of where Billy was and found herself watching him intently and smiling broadly whenever she saw him on the hill. She was perfectly happy sitting there, watching the comings and goings of the chalet, enjoying the mountain view, and sipping at her mocha. It felt good not having to do anything at all. Not having to do barn chores or make meals for her dad and brothers. Not having to worry about Pete who was anxiously awaiting her answer. She had a brief moment of thinking, *Who knows what trouble Pete's getting up to without me,* and happily went back to watching Billy on the hill. After a couple of hours, the group returned, talking and laughing about their fun. She enjoyed her alone time but was kinda wishing she'd gone when she heard everyone's stories, and thought she'd give it a try the next time they went. With everyone else changing and returning their rentals, she was the first one back on the bus.

Happy to see Billy making his way straight for her and sitting down next to her again, Maggie couldn't help but smile as he slid closer to her. He grinned devilishly at her, his eyes twinkling. He had such beautiful, blue eyes. So dark and kind and soulful. Maggie found herself lost in their depths. They had no trouble chatting with each other. It was like they'd been waiting their whole lives to tell each other everything. Like they had somehow always known each other. Maggie had never felt such an instant connection to anyone before. They seemed to share so much in common with their outlook on life such as their love of nature and animals and music. While sharing their stories, their bond grew deeper and deeper. She felt such a natural comfort with him. Both wore a cheeky smile as they spoke and watched one another. She found herself thinking about how soft his lips looked and how she wanted to press hers against his. Longing to taste him, and breathe him in. His hands were so big, she was unable to stop herself from imagining them grabbing her and holding her close. She couldn't help but feel that Billy somehow knew what she was imagining and felt a bit giggly at the dreamy grin he had on his face as he watched her. As they sat gazing into one another's eyes, she felt a pull deep within, drawing them closer. She found him quite intoxicating and hoped to spend more time with him while she had the chance.

They arrived back at the cabin in time to get a late dinner going. Discovering there was a barbecue out back, they fired it up and got some hot dogs and burgers cooking. There was also a fire pit and lots of seating around it, and even though it was cool and snowy, they all sat outdoors in their warm winter clothes, laughing and drinking and eating around the fire. Billy joined Maggie after dinner and they fell right back into chatting and laughing together. Then, as everyone finished eating, people moved around and did their own thing. Maggie and a few others sat talking for a bit, deciding to go back into town the next day and grab a few special things to make a fancy dinner for everyone. They were spreading the word to let everyone know it was a formal dinner the next night and passed around Sam's baseball hat asking everyone to pitch in for the food. After that was settled, and Maggie and a few others tidied up, they all went out into the snow and started building snowmen together. Billy and Jon were working on one that was about eight feet tall. Someone ran inside and grabbed somebody's purple bra and panties and draped them on their snowman. Maggie snapped some photos with one of the disposable cameras she had brought. Sam started a snowball fight that ended up creating a three-sided war between Maggie, Kim, Tina, and Gwen, then Bridget, Chris, Sam, and Tammy and Jon and Billy left to fend for themselves, hiding behind their enormous snowman and using the bra as a slingshot, to deliver two snow-balled attacks at the others. Maggie was having so much fun. The freedom she felt was more than she could have ever imagined. The snowball fight ended when poor Tina got nailed square in the face. She was alright but a few of them followed her in to make sure she wasn't too badly hurt, leaving the others to rebuild their injured snow people. As the sun started setting, Billy was asked by his friends to go get his guitar and play for them, so he went and got it and came back outside, sitting near the fire pit. People just started shouting songs at him and he played one after the other. "Forever in Blue Jeans," "I Love Rock and Roll," "Free Falln'," "Summer of 69," "End of the Line," "Hey Jude," "Pour Some Sugar on Me," "I'm On Fire," and "Angel." Maggie was captivated by his voice. It was so deep and raspy and *very* sexy. While Billy sang, and others were dancing and drinking, Maggie took pictures of everyone. She wanted to capture as much of this week as she could and keep the memories forever. As she watched everyone enjoying their time together, she couldn't help but notice Tammy hanging all over Billy for most of the evening again. Her arm wrapped around his shoulder, whispering in his ear, laughing at his jokes and pressing herself against him every chance she got which was making Maggie feel a bit possessive, finding it funny she was feeling such jealousy for someone she'd only known a couple days. She was pleased to see Billy still didn't seem to be incredibly interested in Tammy though, and she was happy to keep catching him staring back at her. Maggie found herself drifting into one of many fantasies she'd have of Billy throughout her life. As he

49

sang and played his guitar, not paying Tammy any attention, Tammy eventually seemed to grow bored and made her way over to Sam who happily danced with her. They all carried on into the wee hours, again, couples being the first to disappear. Maggie went over and sat by Billy, enjoying listening to him sing. They soon moved inside where they could warm up. Billy rubbed his hands together, trying to warm them at the fireplace. Maggie automatically reached out and placed her hands over his, smiling at him as she softly rubbed them, Billy grinned back. She pulled away, thinking she was overstepping her place, and there was a slightly awkward moment when they leaned a little closer to each other, staring deeply, before Billy held his guitar and started strumming again. Now, she felt like they were the only ones in the universe and he was just singing to *her*. He stopped for a drink at one point, then came back and sat down beside her, and was just sort of absentmindedly strumming, nothing in particular. The only lights left on were in the kitchen, and the light coming from the fireplace. He looked up and grinned cheekily at her, his eyes dancing. She felt a wave of warmth wash over her, and she smiled back.

"You have a beautiful smile Mag," he said. She smiled more broadly and felt her cheeks grow hot. Then, as his fingers found the strings again, he started playing "Ain't No Sunshine" and singing, while looking at her the whole time. She was instantly floating on air. He played for ages and when he stopped, they noticed that almost everyone else had gone to bed. Jon and Sam were watching tv and laughing loudly. Cindy and Dave came down and got something to eat then went back up again, but everyone else was gone. Maggie and Billy were lost in each other's eyes. He had stopped strumming, and they were just sitting there looking at each other. Their fingers just barely touching, softly, brushing together. With the firelight flickering, casting romantic light around them, she thought for sure he was about to kiss her. Their gaze, looking right inside of each other's souls, somehow revealing a lifetime of history between them. He was moving closer to her, leaning forward, she started to close her eyes. She could smell him. He smelled so warm, spicy, clean. He didn't smell like cologne, but seemed to have a natural delicious woodsy smell that Maggie was finding very inviting and hard to resist. Their hands found their way to one another and as their palms touched the electricity was incredible. Their fingers softly touched and tangled together again, and they drew closer to each other still. Inches apart, his breath on her lips, their breathing deepening. Then, just as their lips met, sending shivering lightning through every cell in her body, Jon and Sam let out a yell that made both Maggie and Billy jump, and the two of them smiled at each other bashfully and ended up saying goodnight. Maggie went to bed, lost in thoughts of Billy. Wishing Jon and Sam hadn't interrupted their special moment. She couldn't believe how much she was drawn to Billy. He was just so sweet and so handsome, and *God I want to kiss him,* she thought to herself.

Her heart was a flutter and she found herself smiling constantly at the thought of him. It was close to two when Maggie finally drifted off to sleep.

CHAPTER 4

So, with yet another slow, sleepy start and lots of coffee, Maggie, Becky and Justin, Tina, Bridget, Sam, Tammy, Adam, and Kim went back into town to grab their goodies for their special night. When they got back Sam and Tammy actually disappeared together, and Adam and Kim went over to play on the pinball machine. So, it was Maggie, Becky, Justin, Tina, and Bridget, preparing dinner. Eventually, Jon, Gwen and Billy came to help too. Jon and Gwen started throwing grapes at each other, causing a few others to join in the fun. Laughing and receiving the odd rogue grape in the head, they made their dinner for the group. Becky and Justin were in charge of the roast beef and roast chicken, Maggie peeled potatoes with Jon and Gwen, although Gwen spent most of her time melting on a stool while Jon told her all kinds of facts about potatoes. Billy was in charge of dessert and was at the opposite end of the kitchen, reading the directions for a chocolate cake, while Bridget and Tina were busy making Tina's mom's Yorkshire pudding, to go with the roast. Jon was busy lining up bottles of liquor and pop, putting as many beers into the fridge as he could fit, and had the two bottles of champagne they sprung for sitting in random buckets of snow. Gwen finally came to, lifted her head off of the island sleepily, sat up and made a big salad, then went over to one of the couches, curled up and fell asleep again. Maggie finished with the potatoes and walked over to Billy, who had just pulled the cake out of the oven, placed it on the island and sat down on one of the stools with a can of icing. She laughed as she approached and saw him trying to ice it while it was still hot.

"You'll have to wait for that to cool before it will work," she advised and he looked at her and smiled sheepishly.

"Oh, ya, that might help," he laughed, licking the icing off his fingers. She found herself wishing she was licking them for him. He looked at her with a smirk and she was sure, by the expression on his face, that he was thinking the very same thing. Her body felt like it had filled with hot liquid helium as he looked at her with such intensity. Again, finding it difficult to break their gaze, Maggie tried to busy herself with last-minute dinner prep, and to focus on not letting herself float away. Once things were in order everyone disappeared and went to their rooms to dress in whatever they had brought that they considered fancy, or at the very least, unique for their formal evening. Of course, the girls all had dresses with them, and the guys that had come with girlfriends had good shirts and nice pants. The others had fun improvising. When they all made their way down to the common area, everyone had fun checking each other out and laughing at the comical choices people had put together. Jon, in his brightest tie-dye shirt and bell bottoms, Gwen wore a flowery flowy skirt and neon orange mushroom top, a long polka dot scarf in her hair and lots of bangle bracelets. Tammy was in a tight sweater and leather mini skirt, Chris and Sam in their ripped acid washed jeans, T-shirts and baseball caps, turned around backwards of course. Billy was in black jeans that showed off his ass nicely and a dusty blue Aerosmith T-shirt that made his eyes even more beautiful than they already were. Cindy and Dave dressed like they were a matching set, Dave in blue jeans and Cindy in a denim skirt, both in white collared shirts. Becky and Justin came down in matching onesie pajamas which looked super cute and Kim and Adam in the clothes they had arrived in, which were long johns and baggy sweaters, and had added belts to fancy themselves up. Maggie and Bridget and Tina took a little longer to get ready, having played this dress up game together, a number of times over the years, and finding it hard not being totally girly, chatting too long and having far too much fun getting all dolled up together. Tina had on a pretty lacy pink dress that came down just above her knees and a big pink bow in the back of her hair. Bridget wore a long red dress with a wide gold belt, black lacy fingerless gloves and big triangle shaped gold earrings. Her hair was teased up as big as she could get it. Maggie was in a long black velvet dress with spaghetti straps and under a blue wrap she threw over her shoulders, was her locket. She decided to wear her hair up. Caramel curls escaping from the clip, bouncing softly with her movements. The three friends, grinning and chattering excitedly, went down to join the others. As a few of them found some candles and others pulled a few random tables together and brought the bar stools over so they could all sit together in the center of the common area, Maggie walked around getting pictures of everyone in their fancy duds.

Dinner was so yummy, and there wasn't much left by the time they were through. After filling their bellies, people kept changing seats, so they could get to know one another better, laughing and talking happily. Eventually Billy finally got to sit down beside Maggie.

"You look *really* pretty Mag!" he said to her, that cheeky smirk making his eyes smile too.

"Thanks Billy. You look really nice too." She felt his hand find hers, which she was resting on her lap under the table. He grinned more broadly as her eyes lit up at his touch. Grinning at each other as their fingers moved in and around each other flirtatiously. His fingers occasionally brushed her leg softly, Maggie doing the same to his. Their eyes locked, lost in each other. Maggie thought maybe the kiss might finally happen. Then Becky and Justin sat down across from them.

"Hey Billy!" Becky said, and Maggie and Billy sat up, with surprise, and a little awkwardly, like they were two kids who just got busted with their fingers in the cookie jar.

"Oh, hey Becks," Billy responded quickly, coming out of his Maggie trance. Becky looked from Maggie to Billy and smiled knowingly. The four chatted away for a while before Maggie was beckoned by Tina and Bridget, because they just *had* to tell Maggie that Jon had been flirting with Bridget, and she didn't know whether she should go for it or not. In the end, she of course decided to go for it.

Some people disappeared together for a bit and returned with big grins on their faces, others stuck around laughing with each other. Once it was time for dessert, Billy brought the cake over to the table and Jon brought over the bottles of champagne, and they all toasted to "The Cabin!" Maggie wasn't one for enjoying alcohol but realized she really liked champagne. She actually had two glasses and was feeling quite outgoing and perky. After Billy's cake, they all took everything into the kitchen and moved the tables and stools back to their rightful places. They wanted to clear the center area so they could dance. While people used the bathrooms and did anything else they wanted or needed to do, and were letting dinner settle a bit, Maggie went over to where Bridget and Tina were talking with Becky and Justin.

Tammy was back to sticking close to Billy, who was on the couch, his guitar back in his lap, with a few others piling onto the couch around him. She couldn't hear what he was playing because Sam and Chris had just got the jukebox going, but she could hardly take her eyes off of him. "Bust A Move" started playing and Sam and Chris were up break dancing, Adam and Kim soon joining in. The group watched the four of them, laughing and clapping as they quite literally were busting moves. "Sweet Dreams" started playing next and a few more people joined in dancing. By the time "I

Wanna Dance With Somebody" came on, Maggie, Bridget and Tina were in the center dancing too. Maggie couldn't help sneaking glances at Billy every chance she got. She was completely and magnetically drawn to him. She found the pull between them was out of her control and every time they looked at each other, the whole world around them disappeared. Dancing with about eight of the others, singing along to "Footloose" the "Rebel Yell" and having a lot of fun, feeling the effects of the champagne loosening her up, Maggie's heart felt full of joy and freedom. Then, as the song ended, she felt a sudden warmth behind her and she heard Billy say,

"If I followed you, would you keep me?" She turned around and grinned at him, laughing a little. He looked so gorgeous standing there. His longish dark layered hair softly sweeping his face. His kind deep dark blue eyes crinkled with a cheeky grin. Maggie could feel herself falling, deep. She was surprised by how much taller than her he was and wondered how she hadn't noticed before. Then realized she hadn't really stood next to him yet.

"Ha!" she laughed. "I might have said yes to that, if it wasn't such a crap line." And his head fell back with a sudden chuckle. Then looking back at her with his sexy grin and twinkling eyes, she reached her hands out, and he reached his out at the same time, and the two of them started dancing to "You Spin Me Right Round". She was pleasantly surprised at how good a dancer he was, and happily let him lead her around the room. They were laughing and enjoying each other when all of a sudden, the group over in the TV area were screaming and running towards the dancers. Part of the ceiling had come down in the corner and it was now snowing inside the cabin. The dancing stopped and they all went over to investigate, and Jon, Sam and Gwen started a snowball fight with the small pile on the floor. Maggie grabbed Billy's hand and said, "Come on." He didn't know why, but gladly went with her. She was looking through the few closets they came across and even peeking in rooms that weren't locked, to see if she could find some tools, but had no luck, so she pulled on a pair of big boots and a jacket and opened the door to the backyard, Billy did the same and followed her outside. She remembered there was a little shed beside the cabin and thought they might have some luck in there. Walking about 20 feet, arriving at the shed, Maggie reached for the latch and opened the door. In she went, looked up, reached out her hand, pulled a little string above the door and a faint light lit up one end of the shed. They could hear the music blasting again, "Karma Chameleon" was playing. Looking around the poorly lit space, they found random sleds, snowshoes and skis, skates, shovels, and such, and then finally managed to find a fairly big piece of wood as well as some nails and tools.

"What are you doing?" Billy asked her.

"Grab that ladder," she told him, pointing to the back wall. "We're going to mend the roof if we can." He stood there looking at her for a moment in disbelief, grabbing the ladder and following her back out into the snow. He put the ladder up against the cabin and watched as she started climbing up.

"I have never met anyone quite like you Mag! Such a beautiful woman in a fancy dress wearing somebody's old clunky boots," he said grinning at her and following her up the ladder. Laughing and holding onto each other as they stepped onto the slippery snow-covered roof, the two of them managed to secure the piece of wood, covering the hole completely and climbing back down into the snow together. "And so good with a hammer too," he added as they started walking back to the shed.

"I'm good at a lot of things, Billy," she replied with a big-eyed smile. Billy chuckled. They put the tools and ladder back then Maggie turned and walked towards the door, reaching out to open it. Billy grabbed her hand and spun her around, pulling her up against him. She looked up into his eyes and felt like she might catch on fire. The energy between them was almost too much. His eyes were pulling her in, they were so dark and smoky, and he looked so intensely at her, as he whispered,

"What else are you good at Mag?" Without another thought they were locked in a tight embrace, kissing each other so hard, running their hands all over each other's bodies, pulling each other's jackets off, their hearts racing. With Maggie's arms wrapped around his broad shoulders, Billy picked her up and carried her towards the workbench and sat her down. Maggie wrapped her legs around him pulling him as close as she could. He was kissing her neck, sliding her straps off her shoulders and kissing down her neck to the tops of her arms. Her body quivered, and she felt herself urgently wanting to feel him inside of her. Her hands were now finding their way down to his pants, undoing the button, then unzipping them. They were kissing each other harder again, tongues sliding in and out of each other's mouths, trailing down each other's necks. "More Than a Feeling" was playing inside the cabin, and Maggie knew she'd never forget hearing it in her memories of this moment. Billy lifted her from the bench, and as she stood in front of him, running her hands through his soft dark hair, he kissed his way down the front of her body, undoing the zipper in the back of her dress as he made his way down to kneel in front of her, letting her soft velvet dress fall to the floor. He undid her bra and let it drop, grabbing and caressing her breasts then letting his hands gently feel their way down to pull her black silk panties off too, holding and squeezing her hips and ass with his large hands, kissing and licking the tops of her thighs, running his tongue over her hips, under her navel, then continuing to lick his way back up to her breasts, holding and squeezing them as he sucked and licked each of her now very hard nipples, making his way back up to her neck. She pulled his pants down and was grabbing his ass and squeezing as she kissed him fiercely, swirling her tongue around his. He lifted her back up onto the bench, his pants falling to the floor.

The music played loudly in the background. "Fall At Your Feet" had just started, and their breathing was becoming heavier and more intense. Maggie was now reaching down and stroking him, grasping him in her hand and softly running her hand from his body, right to the tip of him and back again.

"Oh God Mag," he called out, sliding his tongue across her lips and then letting his head fall back slightly as she continued to stroke him. He was so hard, and she could feel the strength waiting to burst from within him. She was so wet, and she wanted him so badly. The two of them were growling with pleasure. Maggie pulled him closer, moving her body to the edge of the bench, and with passion and intensity beyond measure she called out "Billy!" as she felt him push deep inside her, licking every inch of each other they could get to, grabbing his ass again and pulling him in deeper still. He slid in and out of her body, so wet, so raw, almost savagely clawing and pulling into one another, their sweat mingling deliciously. Maggie called out his name, over and over, until she felt his body shudder and felt him letting go, her body quivering with pleasure as he yelled "Maggie!" Now, hardly moving, holding him deep inside, their bodies instinctually gyrating as they came. Breathing heavily, laughing with pure delight, kissing passionately again, still so aroused, they made their way to the floor, shuddering, caressing each other's beautiful sweat-soaked bodies, and inhaling the scent of one another. They lay in silence for some time, then fondled each other again, tantalizingly running their fingers along the curves of each other's bodies. Billy gently squeezed her breasts while Maggie softly slid her tongue along his lips, until their pulses quickened, and they were both aroused enough to attack each other again. This time on the floor, Maggie laying on top of him, licking and kissing his chest, down, down to just below his navel, licking straight across between his hip bones, feeling his body rise, reaching her hands up to his chest and pulling herself up to sit on top of him, her hands running along his chest and stomach, then grinding herself against him, as he reached up and held both her breasts, pinching her nipples as she slid along his hard dick a few times, before letting him slide in. Holding her hips, she let him slide her back and forth slowly, both moaning their pleasure, bending down, and kissing him, open-mouthed, then rising up and down, now riding him hard and fast until he was holding her tightly against his body. Cuming again, Maggie sat up straight with her head back yelling his name, then falling forward to lay on top of him, the two of them kissed hungrily. They lay there holding each other, out of breath, panting happily together. His hands gently running along the back of her body, her head nuzzled on his shoulder near his neck, playing with his hair and kissing him softly. They hugged each other so tightly. He reached out and took her hand in his, their fingers moving in and around each other's, then gripping tightly, as she moved her nose up and around his ear, kissing his neck tenderly.

"Mag, I've never felt this kind of intensity with anyone before," he said to her softly. She hugged him and ran her hand over his chest.

"Neither have I Billy. I don't want this week to end," she said, looking up at him with dreamy eyes. He held her face, looking deeply into her eyes then kissed her so tenderly, she was now melting into his arms. "I wish we could stay together Billy," she said softly, and he wrapped his arms tightly around her.

"Me too Mag," he replied, holding her tightly in his strong arms.

"Billy, I'm supposed to be getting married," she told him. "I can't tell anyone about us." He lifted her chin and kissed her.

"Mag, as much as I wish we could be together, I couldn't be with you anyways. I'm going into the military. I don't even know where I might end up," Billy answered, still holding her close.

They lay there, not talking, the only sound coming from their heartbeats and their slow deep breathing, and the music, now quieter than before escaping from the cabin. They heard "Sunshine" playing and hugged one another tighter. She kissed his neck, making her way back up to look at him, then kissed his lips, so gently, his hands in her hair holding her head. She could have kissed him forever. He held her face in his hands as she gazed at him.

"Well, we better make the most of our time together

than," he said to her, pulling her face close and pressing his lips against hers. They laid there for most of the night, drifting in and out of sleep, snuggled under their big winter coats and a big cloth tarp they found folded up on the workbench. Waiting until the wee hours, they snuck back inside, used the washrooms, and then went right back to the shed, where they ripped off their clothes, hungrily pulling one another in for mad, passionate attacks, then enjoyed more snuggles together. They talked about how they wanted to be together. Dreaming up ways that they could run away together. Traveling the world. All the places they'd like to see and all the things they would do together. Laughing with one another and learning so much about each other as they talked all through the night. Most of all, wishing their night together would last forever.

After laying quietly and listening to one another's breathing, Billy sat up and undid the chain he was wearing and put it around Maggie's neck.

"Mag, I know we can't exist together outside of this week, and you won't be able to tell anyone about us back home, but I would like you to have something to remember me by." She smiled at him.

"Billy, I won't *ever* forget *you!*" and she gazed up at him as he looked at her so adoringly. Maggie reached up and undid the chain to her heart shaped locket, and put it around his neck. He smiled at her. "This is my heart, Billy. It belongs to you," she whispered, and she rested her face back down on his chest as they laid back down together and she felt him kiss the top of her head. They fell asleep, holding each other tight, listening to "Love On a Rooftop."

CHAPTER 5

They woke up, still holding each other, now cold and shivery in the wintery breeze that was sneaking through the cracks in the shed walls.

"Good morning, Beautiful," came Billy's deep voice, running his hand along her back. She looked up into his eyes and smiled at him.

"Good morning," she replied and stretched up to kiss him.

He felt her shivering and rubbed her back with both his hands to try to warm her up. Both of them were covered in goosebumps. She was rubbing his back too, and they were giggling at one another, rubbing vigorously. Then the dangerously hungry stare flashed in their eyes, and they were instantly pressed tightly against each other and locked in a kiss that couldn't be stopped. Still rubbing their hands all over each other's bodies, but not in a way that made either one of them giggle. Billy rolled over onto Maggie, reaching his arms behind her body and moving them straight up her back to hold behind each of her shoulders. Lifting her upper body off the floor towards him, her head dropping back as he kissed her neck and down to her chest, his mouth open, his lips so warm on her skin, sliding his tongue back up to her mouth, he lifted her and pushed her down eagerly.

"Ahhh!" she cried, as he slid in, slowly, moaning "Mmm." Their hands now rubbing and squeezing all over one another's bodies. Lifting her up again, Billy sitting on his feet, kneeling, and sitting her on top of his lap, still inside her. As she bounced up and down, Billy licked her breasts as they moved in front of his face. Then picking up speed and hitting him hard, Maggie's head fell back again, Billy catching it. Maggie kept a steady rhythm, her body landing against his harder and faster. Then with a groan, Billy yelled out "Maag." Both shuddering with orgasm, Billy grabbing her ass and meeting her lips for a slightly moist and very hot kiss. Maggie grabbed his face and kissed him intensely. They certainly weren't cold anymore.

"Wow!" Maggie said, her breath still sounding laboured. Billy chuckled.

"Ya Mag, very wow!" Holding one another close, breathing each other in and shivering again from the cold. They only laid there for a few minutes before getting up, and it didn't take them long before they got themselves dressed and left the shed. The sun was just coming up over the mountains as they stepped out. A gloriously bright orange and red sky was appearing, like water colour paints spilled over a blank white canvas curtain, gradually lighting up the snow on its way into the sky, with a warm golden glow moving across the ground towards the two young lovers. They stood watching, arms around each other, then heard footsteps crunching in the snow. It was Becky and Justin, heading up the drive-way, hand in hand.

"Hey, you two, epic sunrise today, wasn't it?" Justin called out smiling. Maggie and Billy nodded, stepping away from the shed and walking towards the cabin with them. Both Maggie and Billy were eager to warm up again, so they climbed the staircase together, with the intention of parting. Once they were upstairs at the top landing, though, they started kissing and couldn't bring themselves to stop. Finally pulling apart and agreeing to meet each other back down-stairs soon, they went their separate ways to their rooms. Maggie opened the door as quietly as she could, trying not to disturb Bridget and Tina. She grabbed her towel and toi-letry bag and headed to the washroom to take a warm shower. Then sneaking back into her room, she dried off quickly and put on her long johns, sweatpants, tank top and sweater. She was able to leave the room without waking the other two and made her way down to the kitchen to grab a coffee. It was still only Becky and Justin who were up. Justin was working on getting the fire going and Becky was curled up with a coffee on the couch watching him.

"Hi Maggie," Becky said as she watched Maggie sit down on the other couch.

"Hi Becky," she replied smiling.

"Isn't this place amazing?" Becky asked her while looking around the cabin.

"Yes, it really is," answered Maggie, grinning more broadly

69

than she would have if she hadn't been thinking about the night she just had and the morning encounter still so fresh and tingling through all her senses. Justin stood up and walked over to sit beside Becky, smiling at Maggie.

"Sooo?" he said grinning. "You and Billy, eh?" Maggie felt her cheeks going red and wasn't sure what to say, thinking, *Me and Billy what?* Did they know what they had done? Luckily, just then, Billy entered the kitchen, distracting Becky and Justin and their questioning looks, in Maggie's direction. They all looked towards Billy now, watching as he got himself a coffee, singing to himself happily. Then he came to join Maggie on the couch, oblivious to the stares and the conversation that had just started. He took a sip, put his coffee down on the table and then realized the other three were all looking at him. Justin and Becky had goofy grins on their faces.

"What?" he asked his friends.

"Oh, nothing," said Justin, and Becky gave a little snicker. Billy sat back comfortably and put his arm around Maggie and looked at her. He noticed her cheeks were red and looked back at his friends, who were still staring with funny grins on their faces.

"What did you guys say?" he asked them.

"Oh, nothing much, Billy," answered Becky. "Justin just asked Maggie about *you two*." Billy smiled, a bigger grin than he could control, and looked at Maggie again who couldn't help smile, beamingly back.

"Oh, I see." He pulled her a little closer to him, resting

his head on hers. "And what did Mag say?" He asked his friends, still smiling.

"She didn't get to answer, yet!" said Justin, and Becky added, with a bigger smile still.

"Unless you count that huge grin on her face as an answer!" And the four of them laughed. They sat chatting and enjoying their coffees together, nice, and warm by the fire. Then Becky got up to get another cup full and saw Billy's guitar leaning against the wall on her way back and brought it over with her.

"Say Billy, why don't you play us some tunes to start the day?" and she grinned at Billy as she passed it to him.

"Really? No, you don't want me to sing this early?" he asked, taking his guitar from her, and sitting it down on the couch next to him.

"Yes, we do!" said Justin and Becky together and he looked down at Maggie who nodded. His eyes twinkled with laughter as he looked at her grinning up at him. He picked his guitar back up and started tuning it automatically.

"What do you want me to play?" he asked looking across at Becky and Justin. Becky spoke up first,

"House of the Rising Sun," she said. As Billy strummed the first note, Maggie was already in heaven. She loved how he looked holding his guitar. The energy radiating from him was beautiful. Something magical happened when he played it, she couldn't explain. It seemed to capture and envelope his gentle rugged nature, his strong hands, softly moving along the strings, his deep husky voice that tenderly spoke right to her heart. His dark hair, falling around his ears, and his deep blue soulful eyes, looking right into *her* soul as he sang. It was a great song as it was, but she was thoroughly enjoying hearing him play it and singing with that deep sexy voice. At one point as he was singing "Girl Of Mine", a song she loved by her favourite band, she found herself starting to sing quietly along, almost absentmindedly. She never really sang around anyone. Maggie never felt confident about her voice. Her love of music was a huge part of her though. Woven right into the fabric of Maggie, and it filled her up to listen to it, play it and sing it, so she always sang when she was alone or out with the animals on the farm. And when she had time to play her piano, she spent most of it playing Blue Rodeo songs, and she sang quietly to herself then too. She didn't have any sheet music for the songs that weren't from her lesson books, but she could figure out how to play just about any song by ear and in this moment, captivated by Billy, she couldn't help but sing along, her heart was just so full. She was loving the harmony of her voice with Billy's, feeling his voice resonating deep inside of her, but she kept as quiet as she could. She noticed Becky looking at her and almost stopped singing, until she saw Becky smile at her with warmth and somewhat of a cheeky look on her face as she looked at Billy, then back at Maggie. The four of them sat around, singing and talking for hours before the others finally came down and started their day.

Still holding his guitar in one hand, then taking Maggie's hand in the other, Billy got up and sat his guitar down on a chair in the corner, as they walked together into the kitchen.

"Want to make breakfast with me Mag? I'm starving!" and he winked at her. She laughed. They had worked up quite an appetite together and her stomach gave a gurgle at the thought of breakfast. As they made pancakes and scrambled eggs for everyone, they had their hands all over each other, kissing and carrying on, hugging and feeding one another, and through laughter and the odd hungry lustful stare at one another, they gave each other frequent kisses. They felt and acted like they'd been together for years. It was amazing how comfortable they were with each other and how instantly they seemed to know each other.

People came over and helped themselves to the food. Maggie and Billy were still cooking and feeding each other, laughing to themselves as they noticed one by one, people's realization that they were 'together'. Tammy didn't look overly happy, but Sam was, and he seemed to be quite content with Tammy making him her second choice. Maggie saw Bridget give Tina an elbow in the side when they saw them together. Tina jumped a bit and gave a little "Ow" as her mouth fell open watching the two of them. She just stood there gawking, until Bridget elbowed her again, snapping her out of her shock. Maggie giggled to herself. After breakfast a few others joined in to help clean up. Jon, Sam, Chris, and Gwen had been missing for a bit and came in super chill and grabbed the pancakes that were left, heading over to the game room, talking about the meaning of life.

As soon as they had the chance to catch Maggie away from Billy, which wasn't easy, Bridget and Tina went over, linked their arms through hers and walked her upstairs.

"Hey! What are you two doing?!" she asked them. They ushered her up the stairs and into their room and closed the door. Bridget leaned her back up against it.

"What is going on with you and Billy, Maggie? And where were you all night?" Bridget asked in a slightly pushy but excited tone.

"Ya Maggie, where were you?" Tina added timidly. Maggie's perma-grin, growing to double the size.

"Nowhere guys. Just fell asleep… downstairs." Her two friends looked at each other then back at her.

"Come on Maggie!" Bridget said exasperatedly. "We've known you too long for you to think you can hide anything from us." Maggie sat down on Bridget's bunk.

"Okay, okay, I'll tell you, but this stays here, at the cabin!" She gave them a serious look and held up her pinky finger. Bridget and Tina looked at each other again, smiled, then sat on either side of Maggie, pinkies up, and they all linked fingers and nodded together.

"Sooo?" Tina urged. Maggie felt her face going red as she felt herself floating with blissful thoughts.

"Well, Billy and I went out to fix the hole in the roof." Maggie stopped. Bridget was almost on top of her with anticipation.

"Ya, annnd?" Maggie laughed at her friends' faces.

"Annnd, so we fixed the roof." Bridget rolled her eyes at her. Maggie waited a few seconds, deciding what she was going to tell them. "And then we spent the night in the shed." And she sat back, acting like that was the end of the story.

"Maggie! Come on, what happened?" pressed Bridget. Maggie hesitated for a moment.

"Maggie, we've been best friends our whole lives, you *have* to tell us!" insisted Tina, Bridget nodding in agreement. So, Maggie told them. Well, most of it, keeping many of the details for herself and Billy.

"Wow Maggie, I can't believe you gave yourself away to a guy you just met!" Tina whispered with disbelief on her face.

"What about Pete?" asked Bridget, then added, "He's been wanting you two to do it forever!" Maggie felt annoyed.

"Ya, I know, but it never felt like the right time with Pete. I mean, we've fooled around a bit, nothing too major, and it's fun enough, but something always held me back. I guess maybe I always thought...you know, when the time was right...it would feel...more...romantic or urgent or something. Plus I thought I'd wait until after we were engaged. Then we'd finally do it. Then, once we are married it will always be the *right* time. I've never felt that much...I don't know.... intense, strong desire for Pete though. Sure, I like fooling around, and I've thought about sex with Pete, but, I don't know... No 'gotta have him' kind of feelings. The moment I saw Billy, I felt something deep within me, almost pulling me towards him, like a magnet." Tina's mouth was gaping again, and Maggie laughed. "You okay Tina?" she asked her.

"Huh? Oh, ya, just can't believe you did 'it' Maggie." Bridget was smiling at Maggie.

"So, what was it like Maggie?" Maggie gave her a look.

"Come on Maggie, I told you two what it was like with Shawn!" Maggie looked off dreamily, lost in thought and grinning.

"Oh, Bridget, so amazing." Poor Tina's jaw dropped again. Maggie laughed looking at Tina's face.

Bridget looked a little disappointed somehow, then smiled as she added,

"Amazing?" She asked. "Sex is great and all, and Shawn and I have fun, but you look drugged Maggie!" Maggie smiled misty eyed.

"Mmmhm, it was like our souls were one Bridget. It was so magical." Maggie grinned at her as she finished talking. Then before her friends had any more questions she added. "Well, now you know, and you pinky swore not to tell." They went down shortly after, Maggie feeling like a new woman, somehow, as if she had pulled away from her friends slightly. She made her way over to Billy, who was eagerly waiting to hold her and kiss her.

"Hey, who wants to play Twister?" came Sam's voice from the game room. Most people said they would play, Maggie and Billy included. Maggie ran back upstairs and

grabbed her camera. She was nominated to be the first spinner and knew she'd get some fun shots of everyone. The
group took turns being the spinner and eventually everyone
ended up playing. At one point Adam, Kim, Jon, and Gwen
were tangled up so much that no one could make any more
moves and they fell in a heap on the floor. Bridget and Jon
outbeat everyone, and Maggie grinned as she noticed the two
of them making eyes at each other before he tried stretching
his leg under her and ended up landing on top of her. Lots
of laughs and lots of falls later they packed up the game and
people sort of wandered off and did their own things for a
bit.

"Mag, feel like going for a hike?" Billy asked her with a
grin.

"Sure, sounds good," she answered. They bundled up and
were headed outside when Becky and Justin said they'd join
them, and Jon, Sam and Chris said they'd come too. There
was a marked trail for hikers starting around the back of the
cabin that they thought they'd explore.

"Too bad we didn't have any snowshoes," said Sam,
trudging through the snow in the yard. Maggie and Billy
looked at each other with a grin.

"There's some in the shed I think," Billy called out and
Maggie saw Becky and Justin smile at each other. They could
only find three sets, so the two couples went without. The
trail wasn't too heavily covered with snow though, courtesy
of the thick canopy of leaves and needles overhead most of

the way, making walking in boots just fine. Maggie loved the sound and the feel of the snow crunching under each step she took, and the smell of the snowy woods. She smiled happily walking hand in hand with Billy. The sun was glowing brightly, with the occasional opening between the pines, paper birches and ever-green trees casting glints of sunshine along the path. She found herself lost in fantasies of her and Billy walking down the path on their wedding day, then shook herself from such dreams, happy to be with him in the moment and blocking out any thoughts of not being with him.

Bright yellow ribbons were tied around some of the trees marking the easier path and bright pink ribbons for the harder path. They came to a clearing a little ways in, where they found a sign that read the path veering right led down the mountain and all the way into town, the path veering left led to a natural hot spring that was free to use as guests of the cabin.

"Hey, we should bring everybody up here and go for a dip!" Justin suggested excitedly. Agreeing to make it happen at some point, the friends carried on, walking under the 20 foot high trees. They all stuck to the yellow path and enjoyed an hour or so hike together. Jon, Sam, and Chris hanging at the back of the pack, every so often to smoke a fatty, then they'd run ahead clumsily in their snowshoes, hiding around the trees, throwing snowballs at each other between the couples, laughing and carrying on. Maggie and Billy, still hand in hand, stopping to kiss once and a while, but mostly chatting away happily.

"Say Mag, you should sing more often you know," Billy said at one point. She blushed and bumped up against him thinking he was making fun.

"Ya right Billy," she said back to him sheepishly.

"No, really Mag, you have a beautiful voice. It was actually pretty hot to hear you harmonizing along with me." Then he flashed his cheeky Billy grin at her. Her legs turned to jelly, and she smiled up at him.

They came to a spot with a huge tree, its branches extending almost all the way across the path. Billy stopped and grabbed on, pulling himself up and peeked over the branch at Maggie. Totally showing off for her as he did about ten chin ups. Maggie grinned at him, finding it difficult not to be impressed at his strength.

"Grab on Mag!" he told her with a cheeky grin. She stood in front of him and laughed.

"What, to you?" she asked him.

"Yep," he replied. She wrapped her arms around him, and he pulled them both up twice, then they both came down in a laughing heap in the snow.

"Slippery!" Billy said with a chuckle. They embraced with big smiles and rubbed their noses together before getting up and turning back to the path. Hand in hand they started walking again. The trail eventually came back out at the bottom of the driveway. The guys went back to the shed to put the snowshoes away, Becky and Justin carried on around the back of the cabin and Billy and Maggie went inside.

"Hey Mag, meet me upstairs at our end of the hall, in five," he said, winking at her, then continued up to his room. She went up to hers, wondering what he was planning, and changed out of her snowsuit, freshened up a little and, sticking close to the doors hoping no one would notice her from the common room, she went down to the other end of the hall to wait for Billy. It was only a minute before his door opened a crack and she heard him whisper her name.

"Mag?" She went to the door, and he opened it, pulling her inside quickly and closing it behind her. Before she could ask, he had her up against the door, both his hands leaning against it, on either side of her face and he was kissing her forcefully. She grabbed his jeans belt buckles and pulled him tightly against her. His hands were in her hair, holding her head and their kisses became wilder and deeper. He stopped suddenly, looking into her eyes and she smiled seeing that twinkle he had whenever he looked at her.

"God Billy, you make me melt completely when you look at me like that." He grinned at her and leaned down to kiss her again. Just then the doorknob turned, and someone tried to come in.

"Shit!" Billy laughed. "Who is it?" he asked, the two of them smiling.

"Hey man, it's me. I need to get my stuff dude." They stepped aside and the door opened. "Oh, sorry dudes!" he said followed by his Jon chuckle.

"No worries," Billy responded, taking Maggie's hand, and they left the room, closed the door and stepped out onto the hallway landing. They looked around, wondering where they could go, then Maggie pulled him towards the door near the washroom that she had discovered was a closet when they searched for tools the night before.

"Quick, in here!" she said, and they went inside and pulled the door closed. It was completely dark and quite snug, and the two of them giggled before she felt his hands running up her arms and into her hair. Maggie trembled and waited to feel his lips on hers. His hands squeezed into her curls and he pulled her closer, feeling his breath on her face. Ever so slowly, and softly his lips pressed against hers, their noses gently rubbing together, softly, he kissed her cheek, then her chin, then her other cheek, and with her mouth parted and waiting expectantly, she felt his tongue running gently along her bottom lip, then across her top lip, then between her lips and she could hardly stand it. She was grabbing his ass, giving him a good squeeze, her mouth opened a little more as he slid his tongue in and then touched the tip of hers. Flicking the tips of their tongues together then circling around each other, now sucking face, like they had to, in order to survive. She was holding his face too, kissing so deeply. His hand sliding down and grabbing her ass, then pulling her leg up, holding her thigh tightly, and pressing himself against her.

"Billy, I want you!" she said urgently, and she felt the muscles in his body harden as he squeezed her in closer. His hands were under her sweater, softly rubbing her nipples through the fabric of her tank top, then sliding up under it and undoing her bra. He slipped her bra up over her breasts, grabbing them. She undid his pants, sliding her hands down the back of them, grabbing his firm cheeks, squeezing hard and moving her hips sensually against his. He was breathing hard, and she was sure he was growling, making her more aroused than she already was. Maggie pulled down his pants and made her way to the floor, dropping down to her knees. She lifted his shirt, kissing his stomach, then sliding her tongue down below his navel, she heard him moan and his hands were in her hair again.

"Gawd Mag," he said, and she felt him shudder. Breathing right in front of his eagerly awaiting dick, she ran her hands back to his ass and pulled his underwear down, licking the very tip of him as he sprang up. Then she ran her tongue along the tops of his legs, teasing him before taking him into her mouth, and sliding him in, right down to his body and back to the tip, running her tongue along the end in circles before taking him in all the way again. She moved her face back and forth, sliding him in and out of her mouth hungrily.

"Maggie!" He growled and pulled her back up, pulling her pants off as quickly as possible and lifting her off the floor, turning them and pressing her back against the door, sliding right in. She held on tight, her arms wrapped around his shoulders, her legs wrapped around his hips, his hands holding her ass as he slid in and out, quick and hard, her body moving up and down the door.

"Oh, God, Billy, Oh, God!" She was ready to release and grabbed his face and kissed him hard. He let out a slow deep moan, pushing himself deeper, then she felt his body let go and he was back to frenching her, then kissing and sucking her neck, her hands running up and down his neck and into his hair. He left her body, gently letting her legs drop and he slid her down to stand on the floor. Still kissing and breathing heavily.

"Damn Mag! I was not expecting that!" he exclaimed, kissing her intensely. She kinda laughed and thought to herself, *wasn't expecting it either Billy. Never tried that before.* But instead, only said,

"Well, you bring out the animal in me Billy." He chuckled and kissed her again. With some difficulty in the darkness, they found their clothes and got them back on before opening the closet door. Making sure no one was on the landing before leaving. They were both headed for their rooms before going back downstairs, and just as they shut the closet door, Jon came back out of he and Billy's room and looked up at them slightly confused.

"Hey, you guys lost or something? Think that's a closet dudes." And he gave them his Jon chuckle and went down the stairs. Maggie and Billy looked at each other and laughed, then went off to get freshened up.

They could hardly keep their hands off each other for the rest of the night, and at one point, alone on the couch in front of the fireplace, goofing around they fell over, tickling and snuggling and giggling until they were soon making out and laughing, rolling around on the couch. Billy was sucking on Maggie's ear, making her giggle because it tickled so much. He had discovered that her left side seemed more sensitive than the right and was quite enjoying making her squirm. Then, suddenly, Sam peeked his head around with one of Maggie's cameras in his hand, and just as Billy kissed her cheek, took a picture of the two of them.

"Hey, get a room you guys!" he said smiling and putting the camera back down. They laughed again but sat up trying to behave themselves.

The evening was spent outside, barbecuing again, more requests for Billy to play his guitar, people joining in singing and someone made a batch of hot chocolate with Baileys that soon warmed and loosened everyone up. Around nine, Jon and Gwen brought out a huge plate of brownies for everyone and walked around the group passing them out. By nine-thirty, everyone was giggling and hugging, not realizing what kind of brownies they had eaten. No one, save Jon, Gwen, Sam, and Chris, were quite sure of how the laid-back happy atmosphere that had followed their decadent treat had come about, but they were all quite enjoying themselves, and feeling up to doing just about anything. Justin told everyone about the hot springs and said he and Becky were heading down for a swim, whoever wanted to join was to meet them back at the firepit in ten minutes with flashlights, blankets and towels. Billy and Maggie grabbed their things, Maggie grabbed a camera too and stuck it in her coat pocket, and everyone was ready to go in just over twenty minutes. They were moving a little slower than the original 10-minute plan, because they were all feeling so chilled out and groovy from the brownies.

Once everyone was ready, Justin and Becky led the pack and when they got to the clearing, headed left. It was a ten minute walk from the original path, and as they came to an opening in the woods, they stepped out onto a big flat stone platform, with big lounge chairs all around, and a few hanging lamps that could be lit, which Jon and Gwen took care of. The actual swimming pool-like area looked like it had been carved right out of the mountains, and there was a low fence running along on the outside of the water, nestled into the mountain, surrounded by trees and snow. Everyone was in awe and blown away at the natural beauty of this spot they got to share together.

Suddenly, they heard,

"Last one in's a rotten egg!" and saw Sam, Chris, Jon, and Gwen running towards the water, completely naked and jumping in with four big splashes. Everyone laughed and cheered, then a few others started stripping off their clothes and jumping in too. Justin and Becky looked at each other grinning, shrugged and stripped down, splashing next to the already happily naked bunch in the warm water. Billy, Maggie, Tina, Cindy, and Dave were the only ones left on the platform.

"Hey you guys, get in, the water's fine!" yelled Sam. Tina looked terrified and walked over to Maggie.

"Maggie, I'm feeling pretty odd. Think I ate too many brownies." Maggie laughed having been told what Jon and Gwen had put in them.

"Oh, it's probably just the mountain air Tina, come on, if you skinny dip, I'll skinny dip." She looked around at the others still out of the water and saw that Cindy and Dave were now in their birthday suits and jumping in, one after the other.

"I've never gone skinny dipping before Maggie," she said, still looking worried.

"Me either, so let's try it out together." Just then Bridget swam over to the edge closest to them, her gaze drifting slightly, as she watched Billy peel off his clothes and jump into the pool. Looking back at the girls with an impressed grin she asked,

"Hey you two! You coming in?"

"Yep!" Maggie answered. She grabbed her hair, pulled it back, twisting it up into a bun, then knotted it in place and started to peel her clothes off. Tina still stood there. Maggie looked at her with kindness. "Okay Tina, well do me a favour kay, if you're going to stay up here, at least take some pictures for me, would you?" asked Maggie, handing her the camera.

"Okay, Maggie, no problem!" and she looked happy to have a purpose and relieved to not have to swim naked with a bunch of strangers. Maggie dropped the last of her clothes and ran and jumped in. The water was so warm, especially after running through the wintery air on her way into the pool, and the sensation of moving around in the water naked was one of the most wonderful feelings she'd experienced, next to being naked and tangled up with Billy of course. She swam over to Billy and wrapped her arms around his shoulders. He was grinning broadly at her as he grabbed her legs and wrapped them around his waist, then dropping both of them right under the water. They came up laughing and splashing and kissing. Steam was rising off the water as the cold mountain air kissed the surface, and the effect, added to the special brownies, gave their surroundings a mystical dreamy atmosphere. Sam was swimming around, mostly under the water, and sneaking up behind people and pinching their bottoms as he passed. You'd just suddenly see someone's eyes widen and a sudden surprised expression on their face, and the person would jump and yell something like "hey, what was that" or "oww!", every so often and everyone else would have a good laugh. They hadn't brought anything to eat or drink and people had started to get the munchies by the time they had swam for half an hour, so out they all came, shivering and dressing as fast as they could. Billy threw a blanket over himself and Maggie, and they joined the others walking back to the cabin, where everyone quickly went inside. Justin and Chris got the fire going nicely in the common area fireplace and everyone got themselves snacks and drinks. Someone had started the jukebox up and they were all starting to warm up a bit. Everyone was just enjoying themselves. Tina handed Maggie her camera back, but Maggie said if she wanted to keep taking random pictures that would be cool. Tina was more than happy to do that, being rather shy, she found walking around behind a camera made her a little more comfortable.

"Hey, let's get a group picture!" someone yelled and with a little coaxing to those feeling extra stoned and not wanting to move, they managed to get everyone into the open center of the room for the picture. Billy sat down on the floor and pulled Maggie down in front of him, draping his arms over the front of her, Maggie holding his hands in hers. Tina took the picture and then everyone was back up and dancing, or playing pool, the blings and dings of the pinball machine chimed in the background. Some people disappeared altogether. Maggie was happily surprised to see Bridget and Jon going off together at one point, and it was around that time Tina said goodnight, hardly able to keep her eyes open, and off she went, up to bed. Kim and Adam went up after Tina, then Sam and Tammy left together, and Gwen and Chris had gone out back hand in hand too. Cindy and Dave left right after the picture, but they were gone a lot of the time anyways and had finally just decided to always leave the scarf on the doorknob. Now it was just Becky and Justin and Maggie and Billy left on the couches.

"So how long have you two been together?" Maggie asked, looking over at Becky and Justin. They looked at each other smiling and Becky answered.

"We started going out when I was 16, so almost eight years now." Justin nodded and kissed her hand.

"Wow!" Maggie replied. "So, you guys are high school sweethearts?" and she smiled warmly at them. "Did the three of you all go to high school together?" she asked, looking at Billy, then back at Becky and Justin.

"Oh ya, we all grew up together," answered Justin. "Billy and Becky are neighbors," he added.

"Ya, Billy's like a little brother to me," Becky said, smiling at him. "Our parents are really good friends, so we've pretty much grown up like siblings since the time Billy was a toddler and I was just starting kindergarten," Becky added with a sisterly grin. Billy had gotten up and was walking to the kitchen.

"Anybody want anything?" he asked. "I'm grabbing a beer if there are any left."

"I'll take one!" answered Justin,

"Ya, me too please," said Becky.

Maggie got up and joined Billy in the kitchen and found herself a can of pop, giving Billy a quick kiss as she passed him. Billy handed out the beers and sat down next to Maggie again on the couch. Maggie was just thinking about how much she liked Becky and Justin when Becky smiled at her.

"You know, you two are pretty cute together!" Becky said,

looking at both of them happily. Billy wrapped his arm around Maggie's shoulder and snuggled up to her. Maggie cuddled up to him. She was feeling so happy, then suddenly feeling so sad, and tried not to show it. She had been so caught up in feeling like they'd always been a couple, and that they'd always be together, that she had totally forgotten she wouldn't get to stay with Billy, and that she would have to go home, to work on the farm and marry Pete. Almost as if Becky could read her thoughts and wanted to cheer Maggie up again, she got up and went over to the jukebox.

"Say, why don't we dance to a few songs before we all head to bed?" and after a minute of choosing some songs, she asked, "Any requests?"

Billy called out "Ain't No Sunshine."

Maggie smiled, then said, "Never Tear Us Apart." and then as Justin walked over towards Becky the music started to play. "Listen to Your Heart" started playing first and Maggie smiled as she watched the way Becky and Justin looked at each other and then automatically and so naturally started dancing together. Billy stood up and held out his hand, Maggie took it looking at him with a love she hardly believed she could be feeling after only knowing him for a few days. They walked over to the open floor, and he wrapped both his arms around her waist, hugging her closely, she reached up and held his shoulders and rested her head on his chest. He was at least a head taller than her, and she had to stand on her tiptoes to kiss him. Maggie loved how safe she felt completely wrapped and enveloped in his arms. Holding each other in a cozy hug as they danced, she was thinking about how she never wanted the music to stop. "Take My Breath Away" played next and she looked up at him and grinned seductively. His hands running up her body and cradling her head as he leaned down and kissed her, still softly swaying together to the music. "Don't You Forget About Me," then "Every Breath You Take," "Time After Time," "Losing My Religion," "Have You Ever Seen the Rain," and "Never Tear Us Apart." Maggie loved each song, lost in the music and happily content in Billy's arms. As they danced, she fell more and more in love with him. He sang along to some of the songs, and she was entranced once again. Then "Ain't No Sunshine" started playing, and he took one of her hands in his, holding it between their bodies, his other hand resting on her lower back, and he sang to her. Singing like he wrote the song especially for her. She looked up at him, both of them totally smitten with each other, and when the song finished the room was silent. Without any music playing, they kept dancing and gazing at one another. They soon realized they were alone. Maggie had no idea when Becky and Justin had left. Billy walked over to the game room and turned off the light, Maggie followed suit and went to the kitchen and turned that light off too, leaving only the fading embers of the fire glowing in the dark. He took her hand and led her up the stairs where they leaned against the landing railing for ages, holding each other and kissing and saying good night for probably an hour before finally letting each other go, and going their separate ways, both of them drifting on a cloud.

When Maggie went into her room, she changed into her pajamas. Smiling sweetly, imagining Billy's arms still around her. Feeling his touch dancing over and through her body. With each button she did up she thought of one being undone, quivering warmly. Climbing up to her bunk, she snuggled under her covers and re-lived each and every moment so far with Billy. Her stomach flipped, her heart skipped a beat, floating out of her body, and grinning from ear-to-ear as she fell asleep.

CHAPTER 6

Maggie came down the next morning, bright and early, as usual. She was surprised to see that she was alone. Becky and Justin weren't even in their usual spots on the couch. The fire hadn't been lit yet either. She went into the kitchen and got the coffee going, then went over and started the fire. Still, no one came down. She turned around, and her eyes fell upon the piano against the wall in the game room. She hesitated for a moment, but her fingers were almost *aching* to play. As a piano player, Maggie always enjoyed gracing the keys of a new piano if she had the chance. Before she knew it, Maggie found herself sitting on the bench, lifting the fall board, and placing her fingers on the keys. She warmed up with some scales, then automatically found herself playing "Fur Elise", then "Moonlight So-nata". Lost in the music, now playing her favourite run of Blue Rodeo songs, she hadn't noticed Becky, Justin and Billy come down or that they were now sitting on the couches, quietly listening to her play. She ended playing "House of Dreams" singing along, then closed the piano up again and turned on the bench, thinking she'd really like a cup of cof-fee, and saw the three of them looking at her from the living room. Becky with a huge smile on her face, Justin clapping, which made her cheeks go red instantly. Then her eyes met Billy's and the look in his eyes was pure wonder mixed with happy surprise. He flashed his cheeky Billy smile at her, and she smiled back, standing timidly. Trying to walk and carry herself as if she was feeling much braver than she actually felt. Walking into the kitchen, she grabbed a mug and poured herself a coffee. She was hoping the floor might somehow self-eject her into space, when Billy was suddenly behind her, his arms wrapping around her, bending down and kissing her cheek.

"Mag!" was all he said.

She turned in his arms but didn't look up. He lifted her chin and kissed the end of her nose gently, and winked at her, his eyes twinkling cheekily.

"You *are* full of surprises aren't you Maggie Ashberry?" And she grinned at him as he took her hand, picked up her coffee for her and the two of them walked back to the couches to sit with Becky and Justin.

"You're pretty good Maggie!" Justin said.

"Ya, Maggie, we'll have to get you two playing for everyone later!" added Becky.

"Oh, no, that's okay Becky," she said quickly, Becky waved off her answer.

"No, you two should play something later for sure." Maggie looked at Billy and saw a big grin on his face as he drank his coffee.

After coffee, Maggie and Billy made themselves a bite to

eat, then snuggled up by the fire. Enjoying lazing about in each other's arms, chatting with whoever came by, watching the other's doing their own thing. Jon and Sam and Chris were playing video games and laughing their heads off. A few people were playing pool, and the others were nowhere to be seen.

"Wanna go for a walk Mag?" Billy asked, still wrapped around her as they sat by the fire. Maggie cuddled closer to his body and hugged him tight.

"Sure. Let's sneak off on our own though," she answered looking up at him with a sparkle in her emerald eyes.

They put their things on, Billy grabbed his guitar, and they snuck out the back. Maggie looked at the guitar and Billy grinned.

"Thought I might serenade you under a snowy tree," he told her with a wink. Maggie smiled at him and felt butterflies in her stomach. She was so smitten she could hardly stand it. And little did she know, Billy was over the moon for her and found it difficult holding back how mushy he was feeling.

"Hey Mag, how about here?" Billy asked, leaving the path, and heading for a large tree with low hanging branches. Maggie nodded and followed him, sitting down in the snow next to him under the tree.

* * *

"Hey, where'd you two go?" Jon asked as Maggie and Billy came in, hand in hand, big grins and rosy cheeks.

95

"Just went for a walk," Billy answered, his eyes smiling cheekily as he put his guitar down in a free chair.

"Really? We just got back from a walk too. Didn't see you guys," Gwen added, looking at them with curiosity. Billy and Maggie shrugged with a smile at one another.

"Hmm, must have just missed us," Maggie responded. Billy winked at her, and she giggled quietly. Reaching out for one another, holding hands, Maggie gazed up at him with a dreamy expression, her eyes brighter than usual. Billy leaned closer and whispered in her ear.

"Damn, if possible, you look even more beautiful *after* sex Mag." She giggled and felt her cheeks flush.

Around noon, everyone decided to go into town to do a mid-week shopping, and restocking, mostly on alcohol. Some people planned on skiing again, others just wanted to go out with the group. They parked the bus down at the bottom of the long winding road that made up the town, tucked away under some trees in a driveway that didn't seem to go any-where. The group made their way up the road, in and out of shops. Bridget and Tina, Tammy and Gwen went into the lit-tle clothing store together, Jon and Sam and Chris headed for the pizza parlor, the others branching off here and there. They were all meeting back at the grocery store in a couple hours, and when Becky asked Maggie and Billy if they wanted to join her and Justin for a coffee together, Billy answered quickly.

"Thanks, maybe later Becks." smiling at Maggie and breaking from the last of the group, he waited a moment then turned and led them back down the hill.

"Where are we headed Billy?" Maggie asked as they made their way back to the bus.

"Oh, just had an idea Mag." Then he grinned at her, opening the door of the bus and letting Maggie go in first, closing the door again behind them. She stopped in the aisle to look at him, he was grinning mischievously as he passed her, their bodies rubbing up against each other as he made his way to the back of the bus. She watched as he went to the back seat and sat down. Tilting her head, slightly puzzled, she followed. When she was close enough for him to reach her, he grabbed her arms and pulled her close, lifting the ankle-length skirt she was wearing and sitting her down so she could straddle his lap. When she sat down, she could feel exactly what his plan was, grinning seductively at him as they attacked each other. He unzipped his jacket, then hers as she stood back up. Then she pulled her underwear off, and he undid his pants, pulling them down far enough for her to climb back on and let him slide right in. Grabbing the back of the seat and using it to lift herself up and down, he held her hips, his face rubbing back and forth across her breasts, using his mouth to grab them and gently nibble through her shirt, guiding her body up and down faster and harder, until within moments they were both panting and laughing with sheer delight. Laughing and smiling, still sitting on top of him, Maggie looked down into his face with a feeling she wished she could bottle and take home with her. They kissed and giggled at what they had just done, then she stood up, pulled her underwear back on, he did his pants back up and they left the bus, sweaty and happy, arms wrapped tightly around each other, hardly able to walk because they couldn't stop kissing. They walked up the hill towards the shops, in awe of the mountains surrounding them, the snow gleaming in the sunshine, and found Becky and Justin sitting together at a table outside the coffee shop.

"Hey, where'd you two get to?" asked Justin, Becky laughed at his lack of knowing, she herself guessed exactly what they had just done.

"You two look kinda thirsty!" Becky said, grinning at them. They both smiled sheepishly, then as they looked at one another with dreamy expressions, Billy took Maggie's hand and they went into the shop to grab drinks. They came back out and sat at the table with Becky and Justin, Maggie cracked open her club soda, Billy already halfway through his juice.

"So, where are you headed after your coffee?" Maggie asked them, trying to calm down the big smile that seemed to be glued to her face.

"Not sure," answered Becky. "Really just enjoying watching the people and the scenery. This place is just so beautiful." She looked around as she spoke. She was right, it really was breathtaking.

"Think we should move here Becky?" Justin asked, as he glanced around in awe. "We could open our own shop and live up in the mountains together!" and he leaned over and gave her a kiss.

"Ya lets Justin!" she replied, smiling at him. Maggie thought that sounded like a lovely plan and, feeling Billy's eyes on her, looked up in time to see him looking at her intensely. She smiled at him and took another sip of pop. After finishing their drinks, the four decided to walk around town before meeting up with the others. They met some interesting tourists and shop owners, and Maggie bought a couple treasures at the knick knack store to keep as memento's, including a baseball cap that read "Fresh Mountain Air" on the front for her youngest brother. Billy bought a fuzzy blue sweater with a picture of the mountains silhouetted on the front. Becky and Justin grabbed a few postcards, and eventually the four found their way to the grocery store where everyone was already waiting or shopping. Sam was standing on the end of a cart, facing forward with his arms spread like an eagle, while Chris pushed the cart around flying up and down the aisles, the two of them laughing away.

"Hey, we're going to go grab some more liquor," came Jon's voice, Gwen standing beside him. "We'll meet everyone back at the bus." Sam and Chris abandoned their cart and followed. Maggie and Billy grabbed a cart and started walking towards the snack aisle. They placed a dozen bottles of coke into the cart, then grabbed half a dozen cartons of orange juice, about 20 bags of chips, and then a couple bags of ice before heading back to the front and paying the cashier. Everyone was carrying their bags, heading back down to the bus, and once everyone had piled in, Adam started it up and drove them back up the hill towards the cabin, John Denver's "Country Roads" playing loudly. Everyone sang together at the top of their lungs. Billy and Maggie were hanging all over each other in their seat, kissing and smiling the whole ride back. Parking the bus, everybody helped by grabbing the grocery bags, carrying them in and finding places to put it all away. It was getting close to dinner time, so plans were made to barbecue steaks, burgers, potatoes and a mix of peppers, zucchini, and mushrooms. While people waited for everything to cook, most of them filling up on drinks, Cindy and Dave disappeared upstairs as usual, eventually coming back down a little red in the faces. Jon, Gwen, Sam, and Chris went out back to smoke a couple joints, and came back feeling very ready to fill their bellies. Tammy and Kim were sitting together on the couch chatting and watching everyone else. Adam and Billy were on dinner duty, beers in hand, discussing the best way to cook a burger, at length. Maggie, Bridget, and Tina were inside trying their luck at pool.

"Hey nice shot Maggie!" came Justin's voice as he and Becky came in the front door and walked over to the couches to sit down together, joining Tammy and Kim. Then they all heard Jon and Sam yell out,

"Dinner!!" Billy and Adam brought in platters of food and sat them down on the island for everyone to help themselves. People were sitting on the stools, standing in the game room holding plates, piled on the couches happily eating. Maggie and Billy next to each other, in a big plush armchair near the fireplace.

After Billy finished eating, he got up and went over to Jon. Maggie was unable to hear them from all the talking and laughter coming from all around her, but saw Jon nod. Then Billy reached into his pocket and slipped something into Jon's hand, then turning and smiling he came back to sit with Maggie.

A few people volunteered to clean up, Billy and Adam were off the hook because they had cooked for everyone. Maggie and Gwen started washing dishes with Jon, Sam, and Becky drying. Chris, Bridget and Tina put the food away. Soon the job was done, and people did the usual after dinner split before meeting up again out back at the fire pit. Some-one had bought the fix'ns for s'mores, so a few people were toasting up marshmallows and passing s'mores out to who-ever wanted one. Jon walked over to Billy and handed him a bottle of champagne, Maggie realizing that must have been what they were discussing earlier. He went inside, Maggie following him and as he passed Becky, he motioned for her to join them too. Justin noticed the three of them walking inside, following and catching them up, he closed the kitchen door behind them. Billy grabbed four glasses, uncorked the bottle then poured them each a glass full.

"What's with the champagne Billy?" asked Justin. Billy smiled, looking at Maggie, and said,

"It's the only alcohol Mag likes to drink." winking at her with a sneaky grin. She shook her head at him, smiling. Justin raised his glass first, and as the others raised theirs too, he said,

"Well alright then, to Maggie!" and they laughed as they drank their champagne together. Maggie managed a full glass, declining any more.

"Hey Billy, let's get everyone to come in and we can have a Billy guitar request night," suggested Becky.

"Ya, come on Billy!" piped up Justin already opening the sliding door. "Hey everyone, come in, Billy's gonna play for us!" not giving Billy much choice in the matter. Billy smiled at Maggie, as they heard a few people outside holler happily. Maggie leaned over on her stool and gave him a kiss on the cheek.

"Oh, you love it!" she said, and he looked at her, just his eyes smiling and kissed her back. A bunch of people went over to the game room, some grabbed bar stools to sit on, others scattered around. Justin picked up Billy's guitar and walked over to the piano bench and sat down with it. Becky pulled Billy off his bar stool, and he followed her over to sit next to Justin. People were now yelling out their requests. Maggie came and stood beside Bridget and Tina, the three friends smiled at each other as Billy started strumming. He started singing "Into the Mystic," then someone requested "Copperhead Road," more voices singing along, Sam and Jon dancing about goofily. Justin got up from the bench and went over to Becky who had walked over to stand with Maggie. Then, without a request for it, Billy started playing "All I Want is You," and as he sang those words with an epically husky wail, he looked right at Maggie with an intense stare, and her heart started pounding in her chest. His voice was so raw, so perfect, so full of emotion, crashing into her like tidal waves. After U2, Billy took a moment to have a drink, and while he did Becky walked over and sat next to him on the bench. She leaned against him and said something in his ear. He listened, then as she was still talking, he looked up at Maggie. His eyes flashed with such lust she felt her jelly legs kicking in, as usual when he looked at her with such fierce intensity. Becky got up and came back over to stand between Maggie and Justin, resting her head against his, as Billy started to play again. Maggie's heart skipped as he strummed the first note, knowing what it was instantly. She quickly looked at Becky curiously. Becky laughed out loud at the look on Maggie's face. Then as Billy started singing "Know Where You Go/Tell Me Your Dream", Bridget and Tina looked at her smiling.

"Maggie, you play this all the time!" Tina said with a smile. Then, almost at the same time, Becky, and Bridget, on either side of her, said,

"Go sing with him Maggie!" She shook her head. Billy looked up at her, singing right to her. She felt someone give her a nudge and Becky say,

"Go on Maggie." and almost without any control over

her own feet, she walked over and sat next to him on the piano bench. He grinned and winked at her as he strummed, waiting for her to join in on the next verse. A few people clapped encouragement, and she felt herself blushing, but Billy's eyes seemed to calm her and she found it easier to join him, for the second half of the song. He stopped playing the guitar to sing the a cappella part of the song. He was grinning broadly at the anticipation of singing with her. Then, as they sang the first few words, something magical happened. Their voices intertwined together so sweetly. Their harmony was so rich and pure, and they looked deeply into each other's eyes as they sang. She felt like her body was being filled up with liquid sunshine as their voices blended and danced around together. Smiling as they drew each note out from one another, tangibly feeling their souls wrapping together. The room was silent as they sang. Maggie was sure they were the only two people on the planet. Their faces close, as their voices grew stronger together. Then he started playing his guitar again and he turned on the bench to face the piano, she copied him, opened it up and started playing along with him, shoulder to shoulder, gently rocking together as they played the last of the song. They looked up at each other, and as they leaned in, to kiss, everyone was clapping and whistling. Maggie laughed, feeling her face redden and put her forehead down on his shoulder. Billy slipped his arm around her waist and kissed her head.

"Encore, Encore!" yelled Sam. She looked up at Billy and

he looked back at her eagerly, his eyes excitedly imploring her to sing with him again. He leaned his face up close resting his forehead against hers and ever so quietly said,

"Just one more Mag?" flashing that cheeky grin that turned her to putty and he gave her a little kiss.

"Come on Maggie!" Someone was shouting and Billy smiled at her again. She gave Billy a little nod and grinned back at him. Sitting up straight again, he asked,

"Do you know how to play "Tunnel of Love" Mag?" She smiled her big Maggie smile at him, happily answering with,

"Yes." Giving each other a little nod, Billy turned around on the bench again, facing their friends and he started them off. Maggie's heart filled as her fingers happily danced while she made music, and better yet, made music with Billy. Playing and singing, and totally enjoying the moment together. Maggie and Billy snuck smiley glances at each other, her fingers floating across the keys, Billy's sliding up and down the strings. Rocking back and forth in time with each other, a few of the others singing, and people dancing. At one point, halfway through the song, they looked at each other with big grins as one of the lines seemed to tell a part of their story. As they reached the ending of the song, Maggie's fingers gliding with pure joy, Billy's eyes closed, strumming harder to meet the strength in her playing, she felt her heart bursting. Everyone was clapping and cheering again, Billy wrapped one arm around her front, Maggie wrapping both hers around Billy, and smiling as their lips met.

"Beautiful," he said to her.

"Amazing," was her response.

"Play another one!" Sam yelled again, but Maggie was done with her public concert, and the two of them got up and walked over to the group, hands reaching out towards them, more whistling and carrying on, and they made their way over to sit on the couch together. It was like floating in a dream. Becky, Justin, Bridget, and Tina followed and sat down on the couches with them.

"Maggie, that was lovely!" said Tina with her usual awestruck expression.

"Ya! Way to go you two!" said Bridget grinning from ear to ear. Maggie looked at Becky who had that sneaky look about her again, then looked at Billy and realized they had been smiling at each other with some kind of secret knowing expression on their faces.

"Oh, I see," Maggie said, looking from one to the other. "So old friends cooked up a plan then?" she asked looking back at Billy. He laughed, his raspy surprised chuckle and she heard Becky laughing too.

"Well, it worked, didn't it?!" Becky said with satisfied defeat in her voice.

"Get Maggie drunk enough to get her up and sing?" Maggie asked, smiling, "Ya, guess it worked." and they all had a good laugh. The energy between Maggie and Billy was tangible and infectious, and the friends that were gathered around them were happily soaking it up. Separately, Maggie and Billy were both kind, fun, loving people, but together, their love and energy were beyond words and seemed to pull people together.

The jukebox was playing again. People were making drinks, playing pool, and carrying on as usual. It felt like a never-ending dream world. Unfortunately, they only had three nights left after tonight. Maggie couldn't believe they were already more than halfway through their week. How was she ever going to leave Billy? She snuggled up close to him and wrapped her arms around him, burying her face into his sweater.

"Mag?" he said inquiringly, but she just held on tight, her eyes closed hoping to keep any of the tears welling up from escaping, and Billy wrapped his arms tightly around her. "She Drives Me Crazy" started blasting from the jukebox and Billy gave Maggie a little squeeze.

"Let's go dance Mag!" he said standing up and she stood up with him, smiling at him, waiting until he looked away to wipe the tears from her eyes. As they walked over to the makeshift dance floor, he held her arms and looked down at her. She wasn't looking up, but he lifted her chin and when he looked into her eyes, his face became strained, his eyes darker and sad as their gaze locked.

"Mag, what is it?" he asked, pulling her close. She gave him a little smile and shook her head.

"Nothing Billy, I'm okay. Let's dance." and she was smiling at him again. Maggie grabbed his hand and pulled him towards the others who were already dancing. He wasn't sure if they should dance. He was worried about her and feeling like maybe they should go sit down and talk, but as she started moving and dancing to the song, singing along, the two of them were soon laughing and swinging each other around the floor happily, dancing with their friends. "You Shook Me All Night Long," "Never Gonna Give You Up," "Don't You Want Me," "What it Takes," "Sweet Emotion," one after another of great songs, and as the night progressed, and people started disappearing, the songs became slower. Maggie was just thinking about taking a break when "Hungry Eyes" came on. She knew she couldn't resist dancing to this song and Billy reached out and pulled her in, holding her tight. She grinned at him and let him dance her around the floor, relaxing right into his movements.

"How did you learn to dance like this Billy?" she asked him, as he guided her around the floor, doing the mamba with her. His eyes smiled at her, and he pulled her in tightly, slowing down their dance together, as his movements became more sensual.

"My parents made me take lessons for a few years when I was younger. Guess they thought it would come in handy for me somewhere in life." He laughed to himself. She inwardly thought she'd like to thank his parents. Not even realizing the song had finished, they were now dancing to "With or Without You", slowing their dance right down. Maggie noticed they were the only ones still dancing, a few people were in the kitchen, and over on the couch, but almost everyone was gone. She stood up on her tiptoes pulling him down slightly and whispered in his ear.

"Billy, want to dance naked with me?" He straightened up and smiled at her.

"Always!" he answered with his cheeky chuckle. Taking each other's hands, she led him upstairs.

"Mag, there won't be a room free," he said with some disappointment.

"I know Billy, but I have another idea." Letting go of his hand, holding her finger up to her mouth, she whispered "Shh" and opened her door quietly. She leaned in and straightened back up, holding her toiletry bag, gently closed the door, and walked over to hold his hand again, pulling him towards the woman's washroom. Looking behind them before going in, making sure no one was coming out of their rooms, she led the way and went ahead and made sure no one was in the washroom, bending down and checking under all the stalls. She unzipped the travel bag and rummaged around searching for something, then pulled a little dark bottle out, left the bag on the counter and grabbed Billy's hand again. Pulling him over to the showers, and into one of the stalls at the end, she closed the door. Maggie sat the little bottle up on the shelf and Billy glanced at it, noticing it said Vanilla Body Oil on the label. He was grinning broadly at her now, as she pulled her shirt up over her head and hung it on the door. He pulled his shirt off as well, and hung it up too. They stood watching each other undress, the energy between them becoming more electric by the second. Maggie turned the water on, waited for a moment until it warmed up, then flicked the shower on.

"Okay, Billy, let's dance." And he reached out to hold her, she reached up and took the oil off the shelf and with a very alluring look in her eyes said, "I'm feeling a bit dirty though Billy, think we better clean up first." His expression was one of interest and intrigue as he reached out and took one of her hands, interlocking their fingers, and leaned down and kissed her as the water ran over their bodies. He looked intensely into her eyes, as she poured some oil into her hands and handed him the bottle. Then she reached up and gently ran her hands over his chest, sliding across from one shoulder to the other, the water and the oil glistening on his beautiful skin, in the light of the room. Sliding her hands down and around to his back and down to his ass, Billy poured some oil over Maggie's shoulders and placed the bottle back up on the shelf. He ran his hands across her shoulder blades, up her neck and down, all over her back and reaching down to her hips. Maggie purred softly as he continued to slide the oil around to her stomach and up over her breasts. She slid her hands around to his hips and ran her open palms across his cock, then gripping gently, slid her oily hands, slowly, up, and down, feeling him getting harder. She heard his breath quickening and her own pulse began to race. Maggie let go and slid her hands back up to his chest, sliding herself down his body, and pressing her wet slippery body against his, her hands trailing, rubbing and massaging as she slid all the way down, and back up, rubbing herself up against him then reaching up to slip her tongue into his already open mouth. Slowly drawing her body, a little closer, he kissed her, sliding his tongue in. The water poured over them, running down their heads and faces, making their kisses wet and sensual. The water continued down their bodies, warmly, softly, trickling over every curve and crevasse of their skin. Then kissing his way over to her neck and pressing his lips hard against her wet skin, Billy kissed his way up and down her shoulders and up to her ear. She could feel every hair on her body stand up. Soon, their bodies, wet and slippery, were so tightly pressed together. Their hands caressing each other, sliding over every inch they could get to. The warm water running down their shoulders, dripping down their faces. Maggie kissed his chest, running her hand across his shoulder blades, as she started to move around him, kissing her way across his body, her other hand trailed across his chest. Still sliding her body against his, kissing his arm, then she was almost behind him, kissing her way to his back, her hands rubbing his body, kissing between his shoulder blades, as her hands reached around his front, caressing everywhere she could reach, and moving around the other side of his body. Billy's eyes locked on hers as she made her way back to stand in front of him. Her head down slightly, her bright green eyes drawn up with pure desire and vulnerability. Once again, the passion between them surpassed their last encounter. Like animals, they were suddenly licking each other's faces, clawing at each other's backs and asses, pressing each other hard against the walls. Billy's face bending down, sucking on Maggie's breasts, sliding his tongue around her slippery body. Now grinding her body against his, pulling him as close as she could, Billy pulled her leg up and slid it up and down on his hip as she continued to rub her hot wet body against his. Tongues deep in each other's mouths, heads back as they kissed and sucked each other's necks, the water running over them, tickling their aroused bodies and adding to the heightened sensations they were creating together. Billy was now holding Maggie's leg as high as he could, pressing her body hard against the wall, water cascading over them as he pushed himself inside her. Hardly able to hold onto one another, banging her up against the wall, Maggie held onto his ass, keeping him deep inside of her, as they opened their eyes and watched each other. Staring with such an erotic gaze between them, leveling up their already through the roof desire for one another. Keeping eye contact as Billy slid harder, Maggie squeezed his ass tighter. Billy suddenly pulled out and turned Maggie around. Her hands and her breasts pressing up against the shower wall. Billy moved Maggie's hair off her back and over to her right shoulder then grabbed hold of her hips, kissing his way over her neck. She shivered with pleasure. His hands slid up and around, reaching out to fondle and pinch her nipples.

112

"Mmm," Maggie moaned. Billy sucked her neck and slid his hands back down to hold her hips. He groaned as he pushed himself, slowly, back inside of her beautiful body.

"Ahh!" Maggie let out a cry of pleasure, and standing up straighter, Billy pressed his hands over top of hers on the shower wall above her shoulders, thrusting harder and harder.

"Mag, you make me so hot!" he said, almost breathing the words out with a growling whisper, his mouth up against her ear. She wanted to look at him again, but he held her hands, their fingers linked, still pressed against the wall. She was so turned on. His breath so heavy and warm, and his mouth sucking and kissing all over her neck and shoulders as he devoured her with an all-consuming desire. Running her hand down to hold him, Maggie pulled away from him and spun herself around in his arms, grasping him and guiding him back inside her body. Moving fast and steady, almost nose to nose, all at once, still looking into each other's eyes, with fierce insurmountable determination, bodies shuddering, they came together, falling hard against the wall, Billy's body pressed snuggly against her. They held onto one another's wet bodies tightly. Billy reached up and grabbed Maggie's wet face in his hands, kissing her mouth. Maggie hardly able to stand, her arms hanging at her sides, her head fell back with such satisfied physical release. Billy slid his hands to her neck, down her spine, down and over her ass and grabbed and lifted her slightly against him, as he pressed her once more against the wall and she kissed him back as hard as she could. They stayed under the water, running their hands over each other's bodies, kissing slowly. Looking right at each other intensely, licking each other's mouths and tongues, still running their hands over their slippery wet bodies, then slowly sliding his hands up, Billy held her face again and smiled softly as he looked at her.

"I'm not sure how, but you just keep getting more beautiful," he told her, kissing her tenderly. Then Billy reached down and turned the water off. They were still looking at each other so intensely, like they had reached another level of intimacy having watched each other as they made such passionate love together. They grabbed their clothes and opened the door, deciding to go sit in the sauna to dry off for a bit before getting dressed again. They got it going and sat beside each other on the bench seat, warming up again quickly. Billy pulled Maggie's legs over his lap so she could snuggle up against him. Their arms wrapped around each other as their heavy breathing eventually slowed. There they sat for ages, running their fingers along each other's arms softly, gently playing with each other's hair. Then they heard the washroom door open and Bridget and Tina's voices. Grinning at each other and glad they were now in the sauna, they sat quietly, waiting for them to leave again. A few minutes later, their voices disappeared and after a very long kiss, Maggie and Billy got dressed and left the washroom. As they stepped out to walk to their rooms, he backed her up against the closet door and ran his hands all over the front of her body and in and around every curve, kissing her so sensually she felt like putty in his hands.

"Mag," he whispered in her ear.

"Yes Billy?" she whispered back, her legs weak, her eyes closed. He kissed the side of her face softly. Then as he kissed her neck, chest, arms, and forehead, he added,

"I don't ever want to leave you." And they were suddenly hugging each other so tight. Just holding on to each other, hoping if they held on tightly enough, they'd never have to let go.

"Billy…" she started to say, and then stopped herself, thinking he might not feel the same. Or as if saying the words out loud and then never seeing each other again after this beautiful week together would just be too hard. He reached up, sliding his hands into the wet curls falling around her face and held her head in his hands, looking deeply into her watery green eyes, he kissed her lips softly then said,

"I love you Maggie." A smile spread across her face, and she kissed him back.

"I love you too, Billy." And his eyes smiled along with his cheeky sexy grin. She was wrong, he did feel the same and their words were like a magic tonic, filling their cups. They had their regular hour-long goodbye on the landing, finding it harder than usual to walk away from each other.

CHAPTER 7

"**G**ood morning!" came Adam's cheery voice from the kitchen as Maggie came down the stairs the next day.

"Morning Adam," she said sleepily, smiling as she stood beside him to get herself a coffee.

"You're up bright and early," she added, walking to the other side of the island and sitting down with her coffee.

"Ya, Kim and I decided to get up to watch the sunrise," he answered happily. Maggie looked around the common room, and saw Becky, Justin and Kim sitting on the couches together.

"Morning!" she called over, Becky waved and smiled.

"Morning Maggie!" she replied, Justin and Kim smiled and waved too. Just then, she heard more voices, and looked up to see Bridget and Jon coming down the stairs, together, followed by Billy.

"Morning all you beautiful dudes and dudettes," Jon said to the room, and he and Bridget headed towards the coffee. Billy and Maggie were making eye contact as he came down the last few steps and he walked straight towards her, eye's smiling.

"Morning my Beautiful Mag," he said, sitting down next

to her, the two of them leaning in for a kiss, then grasping each other's hands and leaning against one another.

"Hey, does anyone feel like a morning fire out back?" called Justin from the living room. A few people nodded and answered their agreement. They decided to make tons of coffee and pour it into a big pot to keep hot on the fire. Soon people were scattering again and as everyone went up to get warm clothes and blankets, Maggie and Billy stayed on the bar stools holding each other. After a few minutes of quiet cuddles Maggie spoke.

"We could make breakfast for everybody again," she said to him, breaking the silence. He seemed to be in another world this morning and looked a bit sad.

"Sure, Mag let's do that." And before he stood up, he kissed her on the end of the nose with a smile. She wasn't sure how, but she knew he was already missing her. Her heart filled with more love for him. They seemed to have a deep connected way of understanding one another without words. She'd never really experienced anything quite so strong with anyone before. Maggie reached out her hand and softly held Billy's cheek. Looking into his eyes, she brushed his skin softly and smiled faintly, mouthing the words "I love you". His eyes smiled and he gave her a soft kiss, mouthing "I love you" back. Then they walked into the kitchen and started having a look around. There were still tons of eggs, so they planned to make a big batch of scrambled, as well as lots of buttered toast. Maggie noticed Billy was still a little down.

His energy felt very low, so she walked over and wrapped her arms around him, looking up at him with a big smile. His eyes twinkled as he looked into hers and he kissed her, letting his hands drop to give her butt a squeeze. As they pulled apart, Maggie walked over to the jukebox and picked a few songs. Walking back towards Billy as the music started playing, they smiled cheekily at one another, then got to work making breakfast, singing and dancing as they cooked. Billy seemed to cheer up while they worked together in the kitchen and they had fun dancing together as they prepared breakfast. Finding pans for the food and covering them up, they left everything on the island for everyone to help themselves, while they went up and got their warm clothes. Then Maggie and Billy poured the last brew into the big pot and took the coffee out back for everyone. Slowly the rest of the crew came down and joined in the breakfast campfire.

"Billy and Maggie, sing us a song!" Sam shouted. Billy looked at Maggie, knowing she would rather not, but as he smiled at her she gave in, knowing it would perk him up if she sang with him. She smiled back at Sam and answered,

"Ok, but only if everyone sings with us." Billy went in and got his guitar and sat back down next to Maggie. Maggie's heart lifted as Billy started playing one of her favourites, going through the intro, making sure Maggie knew what song it was, then, in perfect harmony, once again pulling the notes from each other easily, they started singing "Heart Like Mine". When they got to the faster part, Billy playing loudly, a bunch of the group was suddenly up dancing. Sam was head banging, Jon and Gwen were moving their arms around and floating about in some sort of interpretive dance and Becky and Justin were up swinging each other around. A few others who knew it sat and sang along happily enjoying it as they stayed warm around the fire, still eating the food, and helping themselves to more coffee. Then they sang "Let Your Love Flow", and "500 Miles," everyone animatedly singing along, Sam and Tammy dancing and goofily walking their 500 miles together. After that, Billy said he wanted to eat, and although a few people were yelling for him to play more, he put his guitar down, got up, walked over to the food and helped himself to some breakfast, Maggie joined him. Everyone seemed to be feeling lazy today. Maybe they were all feeling the sadness of the week closing in on them.

"You two wanna go for a walk?" came Becky's voice from behind Maggie and Billy. Billy looked at Maggie, she nodded, and he looked back at Becky and nodded too. As usual, more people came along, which was always more fun. Adam and Kim managed to score some snowshoes, Tina, and Bridget too, and Sam, Chris and Jon caught up with the group after a morning toke.

"Hey dudes!" Jon said, running up behind Maggie and Billy, right between them, and putting his arms around their shoulders walking along with a big, shiny, stoned grin on his face. Just then, Sam hit him in the back of the head with a snowball, bits of snow flying and falling over all three of them. Jon stopped, turned around, bent over, and grabbed a handful of snow and quickly returned the favour. Maggie and Billy ducking, and laughing with the others as Adam, Dave and Chris joined in the fight, followed by Billy and Justin. The girls quickly grouped together, then without a word ran down the trail, splitting into two groups on either side of the trail, ducking under the canopy of trees and quickly rolling up snowballs, waiting for the guys to come along. Giggling together, watching intently as they heard the yells and laughter getting closer. Jon suddenly ran along the row of trees behind them, Sam on the other side, throwing snowballs at the girls as they passed. Tina fell over in a heap, Bridget pulling her back up laughing her head off as she did so. The other guys were walking down the path, almost level with the girls who waited for the perfect moment, then they jumped up in a snowball ambush. Ducking and yelling, Adam, Billy, Justin, Dave, and Chris, instead of all running away, ran at the girls, and attacked. People were rolling and flailing, in hysterics, legs flying here and there. Billy and Maggie rolled under a tree, coming to a stop at its trunk, laughing with glee, snow all over their heads, falling back down in the snow, still laughing, and lying next to each other. Then, suddenly overhead was Jon, dropping a handful of snow right on top of them and running off.

"Got ya dudes!" he said, chuckling away. Maggie sat up wiping the snow off her face and shaking it from her hair, Billy pulled her back down playfully. They rolled a couple times, scooping up handfuls of snow and throwing it at each other and laughing, then rolling about some more before coming to a stop, Billy on top of her smiling down, Maggie grinning back. He leaned down and rubbed his nose on hers, then kissed her, both of them still laughing.

"We could find a tree to make some music under again," Billy said, giving Maggie his deep intense stare.

She held his face and pulled him close to kiss him.

"Mmm, or we could find somewhere that doesn't leave you with a cold, wet bottom," she said back. Billy grinned and leaned in for another kiss. Then, somewhere in the trees, they heard someone call out "Cawcaw cawcaw", then in a different direction they heard someone else answer with a "Caaw caaw." The two of them laughed again as Billy stood up and reached a hand down to help Maggie up. Then there was a streak of nudity from the woods on either side of the path as Jon and Sam came running down the trail, in just their boots and hats and gloves, arms flapping, yelling their bird calls. Everyone stood there in shock for a moment then burst into laughter again, following along behind the streakers, and making their way down the path. Maggie jumped on Billy's back, and he gave her a piggyback ride for a bit, before dumping her down in a snowbank, and jumping on top of her for another roll and laugh together. Then Maggie got up and ran down the path, and Billy ran behind her, Maggie giggling as he chased her. Reaching her quickly, he tried to hop on for his piggyback ride. She tried her best to carry him, but the two of them quickly fell face first into the snow, piled up in a ball of laughter, people laughing as they walked past them and stepped over them, looking down at the two of them sucking face once again. It was a bit before they got up and continued along the path. Hand in hand, enjoying the trees and snow with sore bellies from laughter. When they finally came out onto the driveway, the sun was high in the sky, lighting up the snow like sparkling diamonds, and they saw Jon and Bridget, and Sam and Tammy out front, building snowmen.

"Won't need to send the search party out then?" Jon joked as Maggie and Billy walked towards the cabin.

"Ha ha," replied Billy, opening the door for Maggie and then following her inside.

The group in the kitchen had decided they were all going skiing and snowboarding again the next day, and Maggie decided to let Billy give her a lesson.

"Really Mag? You'll give it a go?" He asked, smiling when the group asked if they'd join them.

"Ya, sure," she responded with a smile, wrapping their arms around each other, with big grins on their faces.

"What's for dinner?" Jon asked as he and Bridget came in the front door. No one had really thought about it, they were all happily talking and drinking. But everyone was getting hungry, so they soon decided to get Billy and Adam back on barbecue duty. The other guys all went out back to join them and the girls stayed inside together. Maggie helped get things ready for hamburgers, slicing tomatoes and pickles. Becky went over to the jukebox and picked a few songs for them to listen to while they worked in the kitchen. "9 to 5", "I Need A Hero", "Material Girl", "It's in His Kiss", "Gloria", "Hit Me With Your Best Shot", and just as some of the guys were coming in with the food, the girls were all singing and dancing around to "Girls Just Wanna Have Fun", singing into spoons, and using pots as drums, making their best Cyndi Lauper faces. Billy came in, smiling broadly and snapped a few pictures before the show was over. Then everyone dressed their burgers, grabbed drinks and headed out to the firepit to eat dinner. After everyone was out back and they knew they wouldn't be noticed slipping away, Maggie and Billy gave each other 'the look' and Billy grabbed her hand.

"Where should we go?" he asked her. She motioned to the stairs, and they ran up eagerly.

"Your room or mine?" she asked him.

"Mine," he answered, and as they walked into his room he added, "But how about we go out to the balcony?" she smiled and walked toward the sliding door.

"Oh, wait one second," Maggie said and quickly ran to her room, grabbed her winter scarf, came back and tied it on the doorknob of Billy's room before going back in. He grabbed the blanket off his bed, and they stepped out onto the balcony, in the cold air.

"Burr, maybe this isn't such a good plan!" he said, laughing a little. She smiled knowingly and answered,

"Don't worry Billy, I know what you're really capable of. I won't judge you based on what might not be quite as impressive out in the cold. And anyways, I'll keep you warm." She gave him a cheeky grin. He wrapped them in the blanket, pulling her towards him and listening to everyone below. Smiling hungrily, he leaned down and kissed her. She was finding the coolness quite arousing, something she hadn't known about herself before their snowy under the tree frolic, but something Billy had noticed and was very aware of as he slid his hands up under her shirt.

"Wow Mag, happy to see me?" She giggled, but with his hands roaming around, soon found she didn't feel like laughing anymore, at all, but rather more like a woman in need of being ravaged. She reached up and slid her fingers through his hair to the back of his head, and as he opened his mouth to kiss her, she reached up a little further and playfully gave his nose a lick. Then kissed her way to his ear, giving his ear lobe a little bite, licking down his neck and sliding her hands down to grab his ass. She heard him inhale deeply then he grabbed her face and kissed her hard. Maggie moved him backwards and up against the sliding door, her hands finding their way under his shirt and running her fingers along his back. She felt his body shiver, and he was soon kissing her neck, his lips warm and wet as he softly trailed them down, then back up near her ear, sucking her ear lobe. She had reached down to hold between his legs, but he spun the two of them and pressed her against the sliding door. The blanket dropped as he held her hands up above her head, pinning her against the glass, then sliding his hands down the front of her arms, down the sides of her body, bending down and softly biting her nipples through her clothes as he passed them on his way down. She just wanted to do him right then, but Billy had other plans. His face now at her stomach, his hands under her shirt and holding and gently squeezing her breasts, he kissed between and across her hips, just above her jeans. Letting his hands drop down to undo her pants, he undid them and kissed below her navel, pulling her panties down a little and kissing down a little lower. Maggie had let her hands drop down now and she was running them through Billy's hair, her head back against the door, chest rising and falling heavily. He slid her pants down and she felt them land at her feet on the balcony floor. He was holding her ass with both hands, and he used his teeth to pull her underwear down. Her whole body was quivering as she felt his hot breath between her hips, then coming back to the middle of her body, she felt his nose rub down past her wet center as he continued to pull her underwear down with his teeth. Now reaching up, he finished pulling her panties down to her ankles with one hand, using the other to slide between her legs.

"Ohh…" she moaned, as she felt his fingers running along the wet entrance of her depths. He was holding the tops of her thighs, kneading them with his large strong hands and she felt him spread her legs a little before his hot tongue was circling her clit, squeezing her thighs gently, then still using his tongue, feeling her open her legs a little more, he was licking deeper. His hands under her shirt, as he pulled her free from her bra to softly rub her nipples and she shuddered and grew wetter with each swipe of his tongue. She could hardly stand it, and just wanted to feel him inside her, but now he was holding her hands against the door again, and she was unable to move. Billy was licking hard and quick circles around her clit, as she felt warm, wetness running down her legs and her body shook with pleasure.

"God Billy!" she cried, feeling her body convulse involuntarily. She was so close to cuming again, "Don't stop!" she panted and he licked harder and faster, her eyes rolling in the back of her head, then "Ohhhh!" With a long satisfied moan, she came. Billy gently pinching her nipples again, kissing her legs and hips and stomach, Maggie's hands were back in his hair, pulling him up off the ground, her body still shuddering, as he kissed his way up her body, lingering on her neck, sucking and licking, then meeting her lips, which were open and ready to kiss him back. She pulled him so close and kissed him so hard. And Maggie knew he was so aroused now too and more than ready to attack her again. She fumbled for the door handle and slid the door open, backing in and pulling him in with her, stopping as he picked up the blanket, then slid the door closed behind him.

"Which bed is yours?" Maggie asked him, and he pushed her down onto the one he had claimed, standing next to it and looking down at her hungrily. She sat up on the edge of the bed, undid his pants and slid them down and pulled him forward, his arms resting on the bunk above and she pulled down his underwear, and smiled up at him devilishly. Cold or not, everything was still functioning at full capacity, and she held onto the base of his dick, stroking and grasping it as she licked and sucked the end of him until he couldn't stand another second and climbed on top of her, her legs wrapping around his body as he started sliding in and out, almost frantically. Both of them were tingling from head to toe. Billy glided quickly and soon finished off with an explosive yell of pleasure. Maggie's legs were still wrapped around him and squeezing him tightly.

"Billy!" was all she could say, his name bursting from her lips. Their bodies were vibrating together, holding on to one another, panting. It was all so tantalizing and so erotic. They kissed and held each other, the touch of their skin against skin was almost too much, and they just laid there, not moving, breathing hard, until they could finally bear caressing each other without exploding again.

Billy pulled his sheet up over the two of them as they snuggled up close. Maggie's face nestled between his shoulder and chin, Billy stroking her hair gently. His fingers thoughtfully playing with each curl. She ran her fingers across his chest, breathing him in.

"Sing to me Billy," she requested, hugging him tightly. The sound he made let Maggie know exactly the expression he had on his face, and she saw his eyes light up in her mind's eye.

"Ain't No Sunshine" was what he started singing quietly as he continued to run his fingers through her hair and she laid against him, half asleep, smiling, taking deep breaths, and smelling his delicious body. She loved his scent. He didn't wear anything except deodorant, and she loved how naturally spicy he always smelled. He was intoxicating to her senses. Soaking each other up, they eventually fell asleep.

CHAPTER 8

Maggie woke up to an immense feeling of arousal and sleepily realized Billy was under the covers, licking her thighs, his fingers fondling her, pressing, and rubbing against her, then she felt his finger sliding inside her. Thinking she must be having a fantastic dream then realizing it was really happening, as she enjoyed feeling Billy kissing his way up her body, taking her breasts in his hands, and holding them firmly, sucking on them so hard, she thought she might spontaneously combust. Licking each of her nipples fast and hard, with the tip of his tongue, then long wet licks slowly across each one, giving them each, another suck, then back to licking them hard and fast. As he was enjoying her breasts, one of his hands found its way back down to stroke her.

"You're so wet," he whispered, and both of them were suddenly breathing harder, Maggie's body starting to move erotically, anticipating him inside of her. Using his legs to spread hers apart, she felt his hands grabbing her legs, and lifting them almost up above her head, and as his hands slid down the back of her legs, he was soon gliding, fully, slowly and with one long penetrating push, inside of her. As he did, he made a very audible groan and his body fell against hers,

Maggie's eyes already rolling, Billy moving in full strokes, almost all the way out, then slowly, pushing himself all the way back in.

"Billy!" she yelled, and he let her legs drop, and they were suddenly holding each other's bodies, pumping harder and tightly against each other. Their bodies writhing and grinding together. Pulling each other tighter, squeezing and pressing together, moving as one. Then, with a few short hard thrusts, they were finished and kissing, with huge smiles on their faces. Billy fell next to her on the bed.

"Good morning, Mag," he said to her, panting. She let out a little laugh, and turned toward him, resting her arm across his chest.

"Mmm, yes, very good morning, Billy!" and he chuckled, kissing her and laying his head back down, they continued panting through smiles, their hands finding each other and holding on.

Suddenly, there was a, KNOCK, KNOCK, KNOCK!

"Hey, Billy, dude, you guys done in there yet?" Came Jon's voice.

"Just give us a second Jon," Billy called back, the two of them laughing, as Maggie climbed out of the bunk and found her clothes. Billy pulled on his underwear and sat back down on the bed, watching Maggie get dressed with a smile, then reached out and grabbed her hand, pulling her back and onto his lap. Smiling and kissing and running their hands all over each other again. Then Maggie broke free from his grip, pulled him up to stand and he walked with her to the door, looking like a love struck puppy. As she reached to open it, he pinned her up against it, leaning closer as he held her face to kiss her, his mouth pressing against hers, moving his head passionately, Maggie's legs went weak. Pulling slowly away from her, their lips sticking together, then pulling apart, with her mouth still open and her heart racing, he let go of her and smiled, watching as she tried to stay on the floor, while she felt like her body was slowly floating away. With a captivated smile on her face she moved between him and the door and he reached out to open it. He gave her a last flirty look, as she left the room, walking past Jon in a dream-like trance. Jon grinned as he watched her walk away, then looking back at Billy, he gave his Jon chuckle.

"Dude, you dudes' av gotter ba'ad man!" and he gave Billy a little slap on the stomach as he walked into their room. Billy stood in the doorway watching Maggie walk down the hall, with a goofy grin on his face. Maggie reached out to open her door and looked back, seeing Billy still standing there, wanting to run right back to him, knowing if she jumped, he'd catch her, and giving him her big Maggie smile as she walked into her room. He just stood there, staring towards the end of the hall smiling, wanting her to come back. Just before Maggie closed her door she turned around and ran back to Billy. With a big smile on his face Maggie jumped and wrapped her arms and legs around him. Of course he held her tight, just like she knew he would, and they were locked in a deep kiss. As she slid down his body, they grinned at one another, kissed again, then Maggie started to walk away. Billy gave her butt a slap and Maggie turned to smile at him before she walked into her room. Then, as she was shutting the door she heard,

"Hey, nice boxers Billy!" and peeked out to see Kim and Adam coming out of their room grinning at him. He popped out of his trance and stepped back into his room, closing the door quickly.

Maggie was on cloud nine and could hardly even function as she gathered up her things to go have a shower. When she got back to her room, she got dressed and went out onto the balcony. The mountains were so beautiful, covered in snow, the sun shining on their peaks. She wiped the snow away and leaned against the railing admiring the view for some time, lost in the memory of Billy's touch on her body. Closing her eyes, Maggie could taste his lips as she imagined running her tongue across his mouth. Looking back up at the view, she smiled and turned around, walking back into the room. She grabbed a sweater and headed downstairs.

Almost everyone was already down there, eating, drinking, and talking. Some had already got their things together for skiing and when Maggie walked into the kitchen, a few people, including Jon, were sitting on the stools and they were all looking at her with funny smiles on their faces, Jons the most mischievous of them all. She blushed realizing Jon must have spilled the beans.

"Hey Maggie, how'd you sleep?" Bridget's voice came from behind her. She turned to see her friend standing there with a cheeky expression.

"Oh, pretty well," Maggie answered, a huge smile taking over her face. She poured herself a coffee and took it over to the couch, feeling everyone in the kitchen watching her. She had almost sat down when she heard a few hoots and hollers from the kitchen, and she heard Jon chant Billy's name. Adam said something about how cute Billy looked in his boxers and the others had a good laugh. She sat down and saw Billy bashfully, yet proudly, getting himself a coffee. He looked over at Maggie and quickly walked towards her, grinning from ear to ear and sitting down next to her.

"Well, that was fun!" Billy proclaimed, motioning towards the kitchen party. Maggie giggled and gave him a kiss. "Guess they know what we've been up to now?!" Billy said looking back at the smiling faces in the kitchen. Maggie smiled at him.

"Yes, and we also know that Becky and Justin are good friends to you Billy." He tilted his head, raising an eyebrow,

"What do you mean Mag?" he asked.

"Well, Becky's known what we've been up to since the morning in the shed, but no one else has until this morning." She took a drink of coffee, and held her mug in her hands to keep them warm, thinking to herself *I knew I liked them for a reason.* Billy nodded his realization and sitting back against the couch, onc arm around Maggie, he held his coffee in the other hand and had a sip.

A few minutes later Becky and Justin joined them on the other couch, smiling their good mornings.

"You two coming skiing today?" Justin asked hopefully.

"Definitely!" answered Billy.

"Like skiing Maggie?" Justin added. Maggie shrugged and laughed.

"Well, I'm not sure yet Justin. Billy's going to try to teach me, so ask me again later." They chatted over their coffees for a bit, before Adam announced the bus would be leaving in 15-minutes. The four scattered and gathered up their things, and the whole group piled onto the bus. As Adam turned the key in the ignition, "Country Roads" started playing. A few people laughed, a couple complained, and the others were singing along.

Parking the bus in its usual spot at the 'nothing driveway' at the bottom of the hill, the fifteen friends made their way into town, running to and from one another, laughing and chatting happily, goofing around, and eventually making their way into the 'Ski House'. Maggie and Billy lined up with everyone at the rental desk and then they all headed for the chalet, where they pulled on their winter clothes and headed out to the ski slopes. Maggie looked up at the hill that most of the others were headed for and suddenly felt very nervous.

"Billy, I don't think I'll make it down that hill in one piece!" her voice cracking slightly. Billy turned her to face him and pulled her close, giving her a hug,

"Aw, Mag, don't worry, I won't take you on that one for your lesson. I'd never let anything bad happen to *you*!" and he pointed a little further down where she could see another hill with a much more gradual slope to it. She felt her heart leave her stomach and return to its rightful place in her chest. Billy smiled at her as they picked up their poles and skis and made their way over to the chair lift. There weren't many people out yet, so they didn't have to wait long to catch a ride up the hill. Maggie liked the views of the mountains as they made their way to the top and sat watching with wonder.

"Ok Mag, when I say 'now,' jump off." Maggie looked at him surprised and a bit confused, and before she could say anything…

"Now!" Billy yelled, and she watched him jump off. "Come on Mag, or you'll go back down!" he said laughing. She hesitated for a split second, then jumped. They wouldn't have called it gracefully, and both of them laughed their heads off, as Billy came over and reached out to help her up.

"Well, so far so good Billy!" she exclaimed, having another good laugh at herself. They spent a long time, not really moving down the hill at all, and a lot of time having Maggie practice standing up on her skis and working on her footing, getting her used to the feeling, and finding her balance. And although they hadn't tried skiing down the hill yet, the two of them spent most of their time *lying* down in the snow, laughing at Maggie falling over, yet again. Every time she would start moving a bit on her skis, she'd panic and fall over or lose her balance, and fall over.

"Ok Mag, here's what we'll do," Billy said patiently to her, and she couldn't help but pull him close and give him big smiley kisses. He gave her a cheeky wink, his sexy smirk playing at one corner of his beautiful mouth. "I'm going to go backwards, you in front of me, and we'll hold each other's arms and glide down the hill, okay?" Maggie looked at him skeptically as she answered,

"Sure, *sounds* easy enough." He winked at her, flashing that gorgeous smile of his, making her weak in the knees. "Now, don't give me that look Billy, or I *will* fall over again!" and he chuckled, smiling even bigger at her. Billy looked down the hill, then turned back, and held out his arms for Maggie. She walked over clumsily in her skis, stood in front of him and held on.

"Now, spread your legs," he told her. Maggie looked up at him and the two of them grinned. Billy leaned forward and gave her a big kiss.

"Focus now Billy," she said teasingly. He flashed another sexy grin at her before saying.

"Spread your legs, nice and wide Mag," they both giggled, and then Billy tried to be serious and added, "so you don't start sliding, and relax your knees, good, now point the front of your skis together Mag. That's it, make a triangle." She felt herself slide a bit and wobbled, but Billy steadied her as she found her balance. "Good Mag, keep them wide now."

She loved how calm and patient he was and Maggie could have listened to that deep voice of his all day long. "Now, we're going to try going down." This time it was Billy who laughed first as their eyes met. Maggie felt her cheeks flush with colour, then shook her head, trying to focus again.

"Ok Billy, I'm all yours, let's go!" He loved the sound of that, and his expression changed from silly giggles to serious intensity. "Billy, you're making me have jelly legs again!" Maggie told him sweetly, and he came back to Earth.

"Right, okay, sorry, just picturing us on the balcony Mag." Shaking his head a little with a smirk. "Right, here we go. Make your triangle a little smaller, slowly now." She started to slide down a little, then a little faster and she yelled.

"Billy!" he laughed and reassured her.

"It's ok Mag, I've got you! Just make your triangle bigger again and you'll slow down." They practiced her triangle for a long time, eventually making it to the bottom of the hill.

"So, how bad was I?" she asked, with her big green eyes looking at him worriedly, blinking her long lashes at him.

"You did just fine." He grinned at her, staring at her with adoration. "You have the prettiest green eyes Mag," he added. Maggie smiled broadly. "Let's try again." So, arms around each other's waists, they made their way back over to the chairlift, taking advantage of sitting with each other by doing a little frenching all the way up the hill. This time Maggie didn't land in a heap and was feeling a bit more confident about herself. "Okay Mag, this time, I'll ski next to you." They grabbed the poles they had left by some trees, at the top of the hill for her first lesson down. He laughed at her wide eyes. "You've got this Mag," he told her reassuringly and she went through her triangle prep, bringing it in little by little, grinning at him as they slid down together.

"Hey Billy, I'm doing it!" she said victoriously, then suddenly, forgetting her triangle, and gaining too much speed, flailing her arms about, she was soon landing in a pile of snow, legs and skis straight up in the air. Billy slid next to her instantly and gently dropped down beside her.

"You okay Mag?" he asked, not able to hide a grin. "You're not hurt, are you?" he added, moving closer to her.

"Just my pride Billy," she answered with a sad little voice, and he burst out laughing. Looking at his face and hearing his infectious chuckle, Maggie couldn't help but burst out laughing too. He laid down next to her and leaned over her, still laughing. Billy moved his face closer to hers and as the two of them smiled at each other, they kissed, puffy and bulky in their snow gear, trying to hug each other, Maggie, quite literally stuck in the drift she'd landed in, faces breaking into grins at each other, then kissing again.

"You want to try the big hill Mag?" he asked her, helping her out of her body print in the snow.

"I don't know if that is such a good idea!" and he pulled her against him with an arm around her, laughing again as he replied.

"Ya, maybe you're right Mag. Guess we finally found

something you suck at!" he said with a laugh. Maggie pushed him back down in the snow, dropping down beside him and dropping snow all over him.

"Thanks a lot!" she laughed, still firing snow at him playfully. Billy grabbed her and flipped her over, so he was on top, the two of them giggling. Still throwing snow at one another, Maggie had a hard time moving in her winter clothes, so instead, grabbed his face and kissed him hard, slipping him the tongue, and when she felt his body relax, rolled them so she was on top of him and dumped another handful of snow over him.

"Hey!" he yelled, laughing, rolling back on top of her, holding her hands down and kissing her, Maggie still giggling. Billy sat up and they looked at each other with their eyes dancing. "How bout we go in and grab a hot chocolate Mag?" She nodded and while they were already on the ground, they took their skis off and then carried their gear back to the chalet.

They decided they were done for the day and returned their rentals before getting their hot drinks and finding some vacant chairs by the fire to relax in.

"Thanks for the lesson," she said smiling at him, Maggie's eyes dancing as she looked at him. "You're an excellent instructor!" she added. Grinning cheekily, Billy replied,

"Thanks. Can't work miracles though." She sat straight up wishing she had a pillow to throw at him. His eyes smiled up at her as he took a drink from his mug. She gave him a saucy grin back. Billy was looking at her with that hunger again and she felt like they were completely alone in the world. The desire to attack him was strong. Lost in each other's gaze, when they heard,

"Hey, you guys done skiing?" Sam and Chris sat down in the other two chairs by the fire. Billy nodded. "Cool, you wanna get a bite to eat with us?" Chris asked.

"We're going to the pizza parlor!" added Sam.

"I could eat," answered Maggie, Billy nodded.

"Ya, me too," he said.

Sam jumped up happily and announced, "All right, let's go then." Sam and Chris leading, Maggie and Billy hand in hand behind. They were just heading out of the chalet when suddenly Jon was right up behind them.

"Where'r you dudes going?" and they stopped and turned around to see Gwen, Bridget, Tina, and Tammy walking towards them too.

"Grab'n a bite," answered Sam.

"Excellent!" Jon said in his groovy way, followed by his chuckle.

"Should we tell the others?" asked Tina, looking around at all of them. But no need, Adam, Kim, Cindy, and Dave and not far behind, Becky and Justin had just walked into the Chalet.

"Hey dudes, and dudettes, we're headed for some grindage!" Jon called over to the three couples headed their way.

"Sounds like a good plan!" yelled Dave from somewhere

behind everyone. The fifteen friends headed out together, arms over each other, new romances linked up hand in hand, Jon and Sam and Chris chatting loudly and goofing around as they made their way down the street to the pizza place. Being such a large party, they split up amongst three booths, lined up at the back wall. Billy and Maggie slid into a spot first, then Becky next to Maggie, Bridget, Tina, and Justin across from them. Fries, onion rings and milkshakes were ordered in large quantities, and a number of large pizzas as well, and as they shared the food, everyone told each other about their skiing fun. Maggie and Billy laughing about Maggie's lesson, and Becky and Justin talking about trying out the biggest hill and how epic it had been. Tina and Bridget had decided to go tobogganing instead of skiing and were joined by Jon and Gwen. Apparently, Jon and Gwen were in the woods for a bit and came back super chill and ended up just sitting off to the side, happily watching Bridget and Tina slide down the hill. The gang spent well over an hour at the restaurant before finishing all their food and heading back to the bus, making sure no one needed anything before driving back to the cabin.

CHAPTER 9

It was starting to get dark when they got back, and everyone was very full, so there was no need to get the barbecue going for dinner. Maggie went up to change and use the washroom before joining everyone in the common room. When she came back down, she saw a few people had pulled Twister out, for what must have been their 50th round over the week, so far. Of course, the jukebox was playing, and drinks were being mixed.

Becky, Justin and Billy were playing pool and as Maggie walked towards them Becky smiled at her and asked,

"Wanna play Maggie?" She walked over to stand next to Billy, who slid his arm around her waist, pulled her close and kissed her with a smile.

"Sure," she answered smiling.

"Couples or sexes?" asked Justin.

"Couples!" answered Billy quickly, grinning cheekily at Maggie. Becky watched the two of them with a smile on Becky's face. Maggie caught glimpses of warmth and a knowing of their love, on her face as she watched them together. Billy and Justin were standing next to each other chatting. Then, looking right at one another, without a word, started Rock Paper Scissors. Justin laughed as he 'papered' Billy who had thrown out 'rock'.

"Okay, I'll rack'm, you break'm," Billy said to Justin walking over to Maggie again, and setting up, then, waiting for Justin to break, he chalked his pool stick. Maggie had the urge to lick him all over.

"Ah!" Justin yelled with a laugh, not getting anything in off his break. Billy looked at Maggie.

"You next Mag?" he asked, smiling.

"No, go ahead Billy." She stood watching him as he took his shot, and got two solids in, one after the other. Maggie watched him fondly, thinking about how gorgeous he looked, walking around the table, carrying himself with confidence, then whacking the balls with a wonderful clacking sound. He looked up at her just before his third shot, saw the enraptured look on her face and missed completely. She giggled, then gave him an apologetic grin as he walked toward her, scooped her up with one hand and kissed her hard, her feet landing back on the floor again. Becky leaned down and took her shot, a stripe banking hard in the corner.

"Nice Becky!" Justin said, giving her a high five before she took her next shot and missed.

"Alright Mag, let's see what you can do!" came Billy's voice from behind her. She turned to see the look on his face with a smile. She leaned down, drew her stick back a few times, then watched, with disbelief, as she made a combo shot and banked two solids.

"Wow! "What the hell Billy, you could have warned us

she was a shark!" laughed Becky. Maggie looked up grinning, just as surprised as they were.

"Nice Mag!" Billy said, and she felt his hand run across her waist. "So, better at this than skiing then?" She turned her head back quickly and gave him her best attempt at a grumpy look, as she walked to the other side of the table, sizing up her next shot. Not so lucky this time, but almost banking her third ball. When it came to be Maggie's second turn to break, having hardly made a dent the first time, Billy went over and stood behind her to help. Draping his body over hers, his arms running down, over top of hers, and then sliding the pool stick back with her and following through with a 'CRACK', she sank two stripes and a solid. She was having fun playing pool but was loving it even more when Billy was pressed up against her. The friends were well matched, and each game ended very close. They enjoyed a few more rounds together before calling it quits. Adam and Kim had watched their game, waiting to play. The four walked off and Adam and Kim started a game with Cindy and Dave, who had been gone for hours but had finally sur-faced for air. Jon, Sam, Chris and Gwen came down together with their usual shiny happy faces, Sam making a beeline for the jukebox and soon "The Joker", "Jamming", "Last Dance with Mary Jane", and "Magic Carpet Ride" were blasting.

Maggie saw Jon and Bridget slip off together, and Tina go up to bed during "Magic Carpet Ride". Becky and Justin were curled up together on one of the couches, Gwen and

Chris on the other. Adam and Kim were laughing and carrying on while playing pinball, Cindy and Dave, surprise surprise, were nowhere to be found, and Sam and Tammy were dancing to "Red Red Wine".

Walking with their arms around each other into the kitchen, then breaking apart as Billy opened the fridge and handed Maggie a pop, he turned towards her and said,

"What do you want to do Mag?" she grinned at him as she opened her club soda and Billy leaned back down and grabbed a beer, both having a drink while they stood at the island together.

"Well, I don't know Billy, what do *you* want to do?" she asked him, her eyes warm and inviting.

"Jon and Bridget are in my room Mag," he replied, sitting down on one of the stools. She grinned at him, loving him *answering* without actually answering.

"Tina's already gone to bed too," she said disappointedly, sitting on the stool next to him. He leaned close and kissed her on the nose. "So, where to then?" Maggie asked, looking at Billy with her twinkling emerald bedroom eyes.

"Mag, you talk about *me* giving *you* jelly legs! Damn!" and he wrapped one hand around her waist, sliding it down to grab her ass and pulled her and her seat right up beside him. "Look at me like that again, and I might have to take you right here, right now." He grinned his gorgeous Billy grin at her. They locked eyes, lost in tantalizing thoughts of one another, then, "Hey, I know Mag," he said suddenly, pulling her by the hand and leading them upstairs. "Who's in the room at your end, next to the locked one Mag?" he asked as they reached the landing.

"Um, I'm not sure, but the only other people missing downstairs are Cindy and Dave and it's not their room." Billy grinned at her with a flash of mischief in his eyes. They walked up to the door beside the locked room and went in. No one was there, but looking around at the clothes they realized it was Sam and Chris's room. Billy led Maggie out onto the balcony. Letting go of her hand, he walked over to the side of the balcony and looked over. The wall was about four feet high.

"Mag, we can climb to the next balcony. Maybe the sliding doors won't be locked." She looked at him questioningly for a moment, then went over to have a look for herself. There was only about a foot gap between the balcony walls. Billy was already hoisting himself up onto the wall and over the next one, landing on the balcony next door. He tried the sliding door and it opened.

"Coming Mag?" She tried but needed a boost.

"I don't think I can get up onto the wall without slipping Billy!" she told him. His face suddenly reappeared, smiling at her and reaching over the wall, he offered her his hands. She grabbed on and after a few slippery attempts, Billy was able to pull her up enough for her to grab the next wall and pull herself over. Sitting on the edge, Billy reached up and helped lift her down.

"It's not easy being short!" Maggie told him with a giggle.

Billy's eyes twinkled, as a smirk grew with his response.

"Maybe not, but the best things come in small packages Mag." She felt her cheeks redden. The two of them grinned at each other then headed into the room. Billy walked over to the other side of the room and flipped the light on. They were pleasantly surprised by what they saw, and they understood why it was one of the locked rooms. It didn't have bunks, but rather a large, double bed, a couch and end tables, a small TV and there was even a radio up on the dresser.

"This must be one of the upgraded suites," Billy said as he walked over to the bed and turned a side lamp on. Maggie went over and turned off the big light and walked around scanning the room. She went over to the dresser and turned on the radio. Static. She played with the dial for a moment, finally finding a station that came in clearly, hearing "Head Over Heels" playing. She left it turned down low then walked back towards Billy.

"Wow, this is great eh Mag?" he said watching her as she drew near him, then pulling her towards the bed and flopping himself down first, Maggie falling on top of him with a grin. She pushed herself up, on all fours and looked deeply into his eyes.

"It's perfect Billy." And as their gaze grew more intense, Maggie bent her face down, to kiss him, stopping right before their lips touched, brushing her face softly against his, gently rubbing her nose around his nose, then just slightly brushing her lips against his, feeling his lips part, and circling his nose with hers again. Billy's breath warm on her face, he licked his lips slightly, with anticipation, and keeping their eyes locked Maggie let her lips press softly into his. Billy wrapped his arms around her as soon as they started kissing and started running his fingers up to her neck and grasping her hair, then holding the back of her head. She was still on all fours but dipping down close enough to feel his excitement and slid her body against his, then she pushed herself up again, still on all fours. He had his hands in her back pockets, trying to pull her closer, but she wanted to tease him and pushing herself up a little more, almost to a sitting position, she pulled off her shirt, throwing it to the side, bending forward again, her hair falling in bunches of leaping curls all around her face. Billy slid his fingers along her cheeks, brushing her hair from her face.

"You're so beautiful Maggie," he said softly, and she used her eyes to smile seductively at him, her eye lashes blinking tauntingly. Maggie sat up again and undid her bra, her breasts gently falling as she released them from their satiny soft restraints, and tossed that aside as well. Before Billy could reach out to hold them, she sat back, pulling him up to sit, then pulled his shirt off and dropped it. Pushing him gently, Billy fell back onto the bed. Their eyes only breaking their gaze as his shirt went over his head. His legs were hanging over the edge of the bed, his feet on the floor. Maggie slid down his body, until she was standing between his legs, and leaned forward and undid his pants. Billy was looking up at her with such longing now, watching her intensely as she unzipped him. He lifted his body as she slid his pants off. Then she leaned over him again and let her hair fall softly over his stomach, kissing him softly and sweeping her curls across his body. She stopped and held her face over top of his center, breathing long hot breaths over his boxers, his hands coming up to pull her up to him. Maggie held his hands, kissing each of Billy's fingers tenderly and then gently placed them down beside his body on the bed. Now squatting, his feet either side of her on the floor, Maggie ran her hands up his legs, starting from his knees and up to his thighs, holding them, massaging them, and caressing them as she bent down and slid her tongue along the inside of each leg. She could hear his breathing getting faster and she was aroused at the ache and desire she felt emanating from him. His need for her to give herself to him was tangible and deliciously tantalizing. She ran her hands farther up, grazing over his hard cock, then running her hands over and across his hips, she grabbed his underwear and pulled them down, all the way down to the floor. Billy was sitting up slightly, looking at her with fire in his eyes and she stood up between his legs again. Maggie undid her jeans, slowly wiggling herself out of them, watching him watch as her breasts moved gently, and hanging as she bent forward and pulled her pants all the way down, she noticed his tongue run along his lips again, and her pulse quickened. Then Maggie pulled her underwear down letting them fall to meet her pants on the floor. Billy reached out and ran his hands along her sides, and over the curve of her hips with a look of devilish hunger. She reached her hands up behind her head, lifting her hair off her shoulders, letting her head fall back, then bringing her head back up, with her chin tilted slightly down towards him, a fierce smile began to move across her face and flashed in her eyes. Opening her mouth, licking her tongue across her lips, Maggie started running her hands along her own naked body, one hand slowly trailing across her stomach, then up and over her breasts, letting her head fall back again as she ran her fingers over her hot wet center, lingering for a moment to run her finger along herself with pleasure, looking back into Billy's eyes, seeing him sitting up with a look of such ferocious hunger she knew she couldn't tease him much longer. He reached up and pulled her closer, so she was standing against the bed. Billy moved her body nearer to his face so that he could grasp and suck her breasts, his open mouth almost panting for her. As he licked and squeezed them, she held her hair up with one hand, her breasts pushing out more, and she was moving her other hand down to touch herself again. Dropping her gaze back down and seeing Billy looking up into her face, still licking her breasts. Maggie wrapped her arms around him, sliding her hands over his shoulders, she climbed on top of him, and slid her body along his lap. His arms wrapped right around her whole body, and she slid back and reached down to hold him so she could slide him inside of her. He pulled her body against his, hard, and she glided along his lap, moving her hips back and forth. Billy was supporting her upper body as she moved in deep sweeps, her head falling back while Billy licked her neck. Maggie continued to slowly move back and forth along his lap, moving her hips in half circles, as she slid him in, all the way in and all the way out. She was enjoying the slow sensual movement immensely and his arousal was growing as she continued to tease him tauntingly. Then, when he just couldn't stand her agonizingly seductive and arousing dance any longer, he grabbed her hips, quite suddenly, and started lifting her harder and faster on his lap.

"Mmm… Ohhh…" Maggie moaned softly. Billy lifting her steadily.

Then flipping them both over and laying them down on the bed, so he was on top of her, and still gliding inside of her, Billy moved them farther up onto the bed, causing Maggie to cry out almost painfully, and most definitely pleasurably, with a sudden cry of "Ahhh!" as he pushed more deeply with every lift up the bed. She reached behind her and held the headboard, bending her knees and raising her body slightly. Billy pumped into her quickly and ravenously.

"Mag, oh my God Maag!" he yelled, and they were staring at each other again as their bodies quivered and shuddered, Maggie feeling herself reaching orgasm and holding on to the bed tightly.

"Ohhhh!" she moaned, using the bed to push and pull back in rhythm with each of his deep, penetrating movements, and she came. Her body rising and shuddering, as Billy still gliding, moved faster, and she reached out to hold him, one hand clawing at his back, the other trailing down between his legs, finding and softly grabbing his balls and squeezing them ever so gently as he continued to slide in and out, calling out her name with a growl and a smile on his face. He fell forward and moaned satisfyingly, pressing his lips to hers, looking at her as they kissed, their bodies still moving together, then slowing down. Billy slid his arms underneath her, they stopped moving and he rolled them over so Maggie was back on top of him. Their bodies moist with sweat, hearts pounding against one another, she dropped her head down to his chest and laid on top of him, feeling his heavy breathing. Maggie kissed his chest, and hugged him tight. They laid that way for a long time. Billy's fingers lazily playing with the curls hanging down her back. Maggie traced her fingers over his chest.

"Mag, I'm going to sneak out and get some drinks for us," he said after a bit. She slid off him onto the bed and smiled up at him, giving his body a lustful look as he got off the bed, in search of his clothes. He turned and grinned at her, then unlocked, and slowly opened the door, peeking out into the hall. The music wasn't on downstairs anymore, and he winked at her before leaving and closing the door behind. She decided to make a break for the washroom while he was gone, so she grabbed a blanket that was folded on the couch, wrapped it around herself and snuck out and into the washroom to freshen up a little. She was only gone a few minutes and was able to sneak back without anyone seeing her and into the room before Billy came back. Maggie crawled onto the bed and was lying there, lost in a dreamy trance, listening to "Bed of Roses" quietly playing across the room, when she heard him come back and lock the door again behind him. He had carried some pop cans in the front of his shirt and was holding two glasses of water that he sat down on the end table, before passing Maggie a water.

"Thanks!" she said as she took it from him and gladly had a big drink, Billy taking it back and sitting it down next to his glass.

"I think we should hide out here tomorrow night too, what do you think?" he asked, and jumped onto the bed and rolled over and onto her with a goofy grin on his face. She laughed and reached up to hold his face in her hands, sitting up and kissing him, then dropping back down.

"I think that sounds like the perfect plan." And she giggled again as he scooped her up and rolled her back on top of him. The two of them kissed deeply again, rolling about, absolutely gaga with each other. Then, out of the blue Maggie asked,

"Hey Billy, are you hungry?" He gave her a seductive kind of grin and started to move down her body. "No Billy, I mean hungry hungry!" she said, pulling him back up, and he looked at her with a bemused grin, having expected her to say, well, just about anything else, hoping she meant what he was thinking.

"Umm, ya, I am," and he chuckled. "You?" he asked her, running his hand along her body.

"Yes! And I've got a huge craving for a deli sandwich." Billy burst out laughing, Maggie joining in. Then looking at him seriously, she said, "No, but really!" He leaned over and kissed her on the nose, shaking his head and chuckling at her.

"Do you get deli sandwich cravings often Mag?" he asked smiling, his eyes twinkling mischievously.

"No, not usually. Seems to only happen after we've ravaged each other's bodies," she answered with a slightly goofy embarrassed grin. Billy chuckled again and kissed her nose.

"Ok, I'll go see what I can find." And he snuck out of the room again. After about ten minutes, he was back with a few hamburger buns, filled with chicken, mayo, tomatoes and cheese.

"Mmm, these are great Billy," Maggie said through a mouthful. The two of them ate like they'd just run a marathon, laughing and talking away, filling up on sandwiches. Then they laid there together, talking for hours. The music was still playing quietly in the background. Billy had stripped down to just his underwear, Maggie was still naked and just had the sheet draped over her middle. As they talked and laughed, they caressed each other's bodies, memorizing every line, curve, and crevice. Soaking up the feel and smell and every detail of their young smooth, taught bodies and storing the images deep in their minds. Eventually they drifted off to sleep, still wrapped in each other's arms.

CHAPTER 10

"Billy," Maggie whispered, sometime near five the next morning.

"Huhh?" came Billy's sleepy grumble.

"Billy," she said again, leaning over and kissing him. As he was waking up, he kissed her back, then squinted up at her.

"What's up Mag?" she grinned at him.

"Let's go watch the sunrise." He stretched his arms above his head on the bed.

"Ok," he answered very sleepily, eyes closed, and smiling at her. They found their clothes and got dressed. Maggie was cold though, and only had her T-shirt, so Billy handed her the fuzzy blue sweater he'd bought at the little store in town. She smiled, and pulled it over her head, happily smelling it.

"Thanks Billy, that's better." He winked and smiled at her. Now ready to make their way out of their secret oasis, they kept the door locked, and went out to the balcony. The two of them giggling as they tried to quietly climb the wall, half asleep. Billy helped her down again and slowly and as quietly as they could, sliding the balcony door open, went back into Chris and Sam's room, then slowly and quietly sliding it closed, Maggie covered her mouth to stifle her giggles, they walked to the other side of the room, slipped out and closed the door behind them.

"Meet you downstairs in a few?" she said to him, he nodded, and they went to their rooms to get their winter coats and a blanket each and stop by the washrooms before heading down to the common room. Maggie was downstairs first and decided to put the coffee on, in hopes there'd still be some when they came back in. She turned around when she heard the stairs creak and saw Billy's grinning face come around the railing.

"Ready Mag?" He asked, walking up to her, his blanket already draped around his shoulders, and as he drew closer, he opened his arms and pulled her in and under the blanket with him, leaning down and pressing his lips softly to hers. Her eyes sparkled as she looked up at him. They broke apart and pulled their hats and gloves and boots on, then headed out the front door. The sky was already brightening slightly but they couldn't see the sun yet, so hand in hand they walked down the driveway in hopes of finding the perfect spot to sit and wait. It was snowing very softly and the tiny flakes sparkled in the light of the new day. They came to a place with a fallen tree they could sit on, and sitting next to each other, they saw there was just enough space through the distant forest trees for them to watch the light starting to come up behind the mountains. At first, just a bright ribbon of golden light stretched across the outline of the mountains, then the sun, coral, and gold began to light up the mountains in a dazzling blanket of beauty. Bringing each nook and cranny into sudden vibrant light, illuminating the depth and layers of the rocks as it rose higher. Maggie and Billy sat, wrapped cozily, snuggled up together with Billy's arm around her shoulder, her head resting against his chest. They didn't speak as they watched, sitting quietly in awe. Soon, the sun became so bright, they could hardly see the mountains from the bright glare. Billy reached up with his free hand and held her face, a grin playing around one corner of his lips. She looked at the lines around his mouth and thought about how much she loved him. How she knew she'd never forget the way his eyes crinkled when he smiled at her. The dark blue of his eyes, so deep and loving, made her feel like she was falling right into them, like being submerged in a deep warm pool of water. She felt so safe and able to be herself with him. The sun was now shining on the driveway and casting shimmering light onto the snow and across Maggie's face. Billy smiled at her and couldn't help but get lost in her sparkling emerald eyes that always seemed to light up when she looked at him. Loving her huge, beautiful smile, that somehow made him feel like he was home. The way her skin always smelled of vanilla and her hair like lavender even when she wasn't wearing them. Their faces drew closer, looking into each other's eyes, the sunlight catching the thread of caramel highlights woven into the curls that were escaping beneath her hat. He smiled at her again, then slowly, closing her eyes, she felt his warm breath on her lips, before he, ever so softly, with his lips gently parting, kissed her mouth with such tenderness. Their mouths hardly pressing together, their lips lightly pulling away, almost whispering their touch. And then both inhaling deeply, they were pressed together, moving more passionately, holding each other tight. The sun, shining bright and warm on their faces. A moment she would forever keep in her heart, and one she hoped he would too. Pulling apart and smiling as they looked back into each other's eyes, they heard footsteps crunching in the snow and looked down the driveway to see Becky and Justin walking up hand in hand.

"Good morning love birds!" came Justin's usual bemused voice. Becky smiled broadly at the two of them.

"Morning," Maggie and Billy said with big grins.

"What a sunrise this morning!" said Justin with fascination on his face. "Never get tired of that!" he added, looking lovingly at Becky. Maggie and Billy stood up and joined them, walking back to the cabin together.

No one else was up yet, and the four were very happy to come back in from the cold, to Maggie's freshly brewed coffee. Justin got the fire going and the four of them took up their usual morning spots together on the couches. Billy had sat down against the arm of the couch with his legs running the length, and Maggie sat along beside him, cozied up against his warm body.

"So, what's the plan today?" asked Justin as he finished with the fire and sat down next to Becky. Billy shrugged, and

Maggie snuggled up closer to him.

"I know there's a big bash planned for tonight," Billy answered, "Finish the food and alcohol and blast some tunes," he added.

"But of course!" said Justin, smiling.

"Goood morning dudes and dudettes!" came Jon's happy laid-back morning salutations to the others.

"Morning," the four shouted back.

"So, what's happening for our last righteous day?" Laughing, Justin told him they were just wondering the same thing. And as they tried to come up with a plan, people started appearing and sitting here and there, adding their own thoughts on the subject. Surprisingly, everyone was up relatively early, hoping to get the most out of the last full day together. Drinking coffee and trying to wake up as much as they could, they all added their two cents for what they thought they should do. The party that night was a given, so there was no need for them to discuss that, but everyone wanted to do something different for their day together.

Finally, after continued indecision, Jon stood up on the coffee table and speaking to the whole room at large, announced,

"Ok dudes and dudettes, the deal is, we do it all!!" ending with his classic chuckle. That meant, big breakfast, twister, charades, pool, building snowmen, barbecuing, Billy playing his guitar, any skits or acts a few of them had planned, drinking and more drinking, then the epic all night party, and of course, at least one quicky break for Cindy and Dave.

Billy, Maggie, Becky, Justin, Kim, and Adam made their way to the kitchen and pulled everything out from the fridge and cupboards, and setting aside anything that could be classified as 'breakfast', which meant eggs, pancakes, waffles, french toast, regular toast, cereal, fruit, bacon, sausages, and more coffee with the last of the Baileys in it and with two full cartons of orange juice, there was a request for mimosas. Chris and Sam, along with Tammy and Bridget said they'd go get more champagne, so Adam and Kim joined them, as Adam was the designated bus driver. They left right away so they could get back with the champagne in time for breakfast.

As they started preparing everything for their brunch, Tina, Gwen, Cindy, Dave, Jon, and Bridget moved all the tables together again, brought the stools over and sat them at the tables, and finding the last of the condiments, jam and peanut butter, honey, syrup, plates and cutlery, brought them over to the table too. Just as the bus crew came back with two bottles of champagne and one more two-four for later, the kitchen crew was bringing the food over to the table, where everyone sat down together, hungry, happy and ready to eat. Jon and Sam finished eating and entertained the group with a ventriloquist and dummy act. Jon was sitting on Sam's lap as the doll. They had everyone in hysterics with their goofy act. Gwen and Tammy sang and danced and acted out a visual rendition of "I've Got a Brand New Pair of

Roller Skates". Gwen pretending to be on her roller skates, and Sam and Chris filling in as Tammy's bicycle, which was absolutely hilarious. Then they were hollering for Billy to do requests for them. He said he'd sing four songs tops, and everyone agreed as long as Maggie did a 5th one with him. Luckily for them she was on her 3rd mimosa and was more than happy to sing along.

They got Billy to sing "More Than Words", "November Rain", which made Maggie melt on the spot, "The Gambler", and "Me and Bobby Mcgee". Then they coaxed Maggie up and got the two lovebirds to sing "I Got You Babe" which ended up being super cute and everyone clapped and eww'd and aww'd at them. After the serenade, they cleaned up the dishes and cleared the center floor. With everyone helping, they finished in no time. Moving the tables and stools back, everyone felt like lazing about, so they all agreed to take a half hour of 'do your own thing' time.

"So Cindy and Dave don't die from not doing it!" yelled Sam, to lots of laughter, and laughing even harder when they all saw them climbing the staircase together. Jon, Chris, Gwen, and Sam went out back to smoke a couple joints together. Becky and Justin went for a short walk, on the trails. Tina, Bridget, Tammy, Kim, and Adam went out front to build snowmen and Billy and Maggie curled up in front of the fire. Deep into one of their make-out sessions until the stoner crew came back in. So Maggie and Billy decided to go play a game of pool together. Billy racked up the balls and throwing Maggie a saucy grin, said,

"You wanna break'em Beautiful?" knowing she couldn't and would want his help. She looked at him, knowing what he was thinking, and smiled back devilishly and replied,

"Nahh." He looked shocked for a moment, then chuckling walked over to her, dipping her and kissing her hard, so when she stood up, she was slightly dazed. She laughed and walked over to break. "Oh Billy, won't you please help me?" she asked in a sweet Marilyn like voice. He grinned, and strutting cutely, walked behind her, gave her a little push from his hips, causing her to stand up straight with happy shock, and then hearing him laugh, she bent over the table again, and pressed her bottom against him and wiggled her hips.

"Oh my!" he said, and she giggled. He leaned over her, arms wrapped around her, and leaned his face down near her ear and said, "On the stroke of three Mag." and they slid the stick back and forth, then... CRACK! Sinking a stripe in the far corner. When Maggie tried to stand back up though, Billy stayed draped over her.

"Billy!" she said playfully, and he moved just enough for her to stand up, having to tightly squeeze her body out from between him and the table. He bent down and kissed her and winked as she freed herself. "You're not trying to win this game by distracting me are you, Billy Stanton?" His eyes flashed with mischief,

"Now Mag, would I do a thing like that?" She walked

around the table to take her next shot, steadied herself, leaning forward on the table so her shirt hung open for him to get a clear view, she pulled her stick back, and right before making the shot, lifted her eyes to look at him, licked her lips and followed through, banking another stripe. His mouth hanging open for a second then his head falling back with his deep Billy chuckle. She walked towards him and bent over the table right in front of him. Her butt up as much as possible, and giving it a little shake, she sunk another ball.

"Whoa, I think Mimosas are your rocket fuel!" he said with a surprised look on his face.

"You're my rocket fuel Billy!" Maggie's eyes gazing sensually at him, reaching around, and squeezing his butt. She banked one more before she finished her turn. Billy found his next shot and as he leaned forward to take it, she leaned forward opposite him, pulled her shirt down and mouthed,

"I want you," giggling as he grazed the cue ball and missed his shot.

"Oh, Mag!" he said, laughing, and running after her. She ran around the table and was already banking another ball before he got to her. He picked her up and spun, the two of them laughing. Then, as she was ready to shoot, Billy leaned close, sticking his face into her hair and sticking his tongue in her ear. She missed the shot completely.

"Ok Billy, I didn't want to show you up, so if you want, I'll let you get a couple in," she told him cheekily, and he shook his head at her and grinned. He did bank the next two, but she couldn't resist messing with his next shot. Before he went for it, he looked at her, waiting for her to try something. She shrugged innocently, then he bent forward and was just ready to hit the cue ball. She laid her upper body on the table across from him, stuck her finger in her mouth and licked it as she moved it in and out. He tilted his head with a sound of arousal, and laughed, standing back up without taking his turn. She stood up and grinned. Then ran over to him and stood on her tippy toes to give him a long kiss. They didn't end up finishing their game of pool, still sucking face, leaning against the pool table, when everyone came back, but they were certainly thinking about finishing the other game they'd been playing, when they had their chance later.

The afternoon was spent playing charades and Twister. They split up into girls against guys for charades and the girls smoked them. The guys yelled 'rigged' at them when they claimed victory. Jon won the final battle of Twister. Being the tallest and skinniest was very useful for Twister. By that time, some people were wanting to play some drinking games. Billy found a half-empty bottle of champagne still left from breakfast and kept it nearby for Maggie. They settled on Sam's favourite drinking game, known by him as the '30-second drinking game.' Two people would face off, one person describing, in rhyming words or sounds, a random word they couldn't say, and the other person had to guess what it was. If they couldn't guess in 30 -seconds, they had to have a shot of vodka, or in Maggie's case, a swig of champagne.

That kept them busy for a while, until all the champagne and vodka was gone. Then they headed out back to the fire pit and got an early dinner going. It was pretty random, with a few leftovers from some of their dinners from the week. It started snowing while they were out there, and it was absolutely beautiful. Watching as it was gently falling, dusting the back patio and everyone's hats and heads in big fluffy snowflakes. The view of the mountains in the background and the fire blazing in the pit made the evening just that much more magical for The Cabiners.

Half the group decided to go skating on the rink in the backyard while the others got the leftovers ready. Maggie and Billy floated along together like they were on a cloud. Maggie spent a lot of time on backyard rinks growing up and Billy had played hockey for most of his life. They moved together flawlessly, holding tight and gliding happily. Eventually, working up an appetite, they joined the others who were already eating. After dinner, they had another half-hour break, for Cindy and Dave, then came back for dancing and more drinking. The two-four was opened and was soon finished. Maggie and Billy were up dancing with half the group. Neither one of them had any more alcohol after dinner and were quite content to twirl and move each other around the dance floor. "Mr. Blue Sky" started playing and everyone was up singing and dancing. Sam bouncing around everyone goofily, grabbing Tammy and dancing her around with him. Becky and Justin doing the tango through the center of the dancers. "Poison" came on and a few of the guys couldn't help but play their air guitars for their girls, doing their best imitations of Alice. When "Romeo and Juliet" started, Maggie grabbed Billy's hand and pulled him in close. He held her tight, his hands in her back jeans' pockets, hers in his, looking up at him as he sang along quietly, looking down into her eyes.

It was only about ten when the two of them snuck off together, grabbing the last few club sodas and a couple of beers and heading upstairs together. As they passed Sam and Chris and Jon in the kitchen they heard "Ooooh" and kissy noises. They smiled at each other as they continued up to the landing.

"I'm just going to freshen up a bit Billy," she said as they kissed against the railing at the top.

"Okay Beautiful, back in five." And he turned to walk down the hall. She decided on a quick visit to the bathroom. Then she went back out to meet him on the landing. There was nothing hanging on Sam and Chris's doorknob, so they went in, and headed for the balcony, Billy climbing over first, taking their drinks then pulling Maggie up and helping her over. Billy slid the doors open and they went in, carefully crossing the dark room to find the lamp, Maggie switched it on. Then both of them flopped down and landed side by side on the bed.

CHAPTER 11

"Wow, what a day!" Maggie said, smiling from ear to ear. Billy turned over on his side and slid his hand across her stomach, under her shirt and ran his hand around her belly and abdomen, looking at her. She turned her head and looked into his now serious, and deeper and dreamier than usual, dark blue eyes.

"Luckily, the day's not over yet Mag," he breathed. She rolled onto her side and gently touched his cheek, softly running her fingers over his lips, as they gazed at one another. Then she held his face in her hand. He closed his eyes as he smiled, and she moved closer to kiss him, her hand now sliding back, into his hair, his free hand doing the same, and gently grasping her curls in his hand to pull her in closer and kiss her harder. Soon tongues were going, and their breathing grew heavier, moving into each other slowly and deeply. They unlocked and looked at each other again. Billy sat up, pulling Maggie up with him, then he stood up and reached out his hand, she took it, and he pulled her up into his arms.

"Dance with me," he said in a whisper, moving them away from the bed. They could only faintly hear the music from downstairs, and Maggie said,

"We don't have any music, I'll turn the radio on." Billy pulled her up to him tight and replied.

"Let's make our own music Mag." And she felt her legs give out. He held one of her hands, placed her other hand on his shoulder and then slid his hand down to the bottom of her back. Looking right into her eyes, he stepped one foot back, guiding her. She stepped her foot forward, then he stepped his foot forward, moving her backwards and she stepped her foot back.

She saw him grin, as he said, "That's it, Mag, just let me lead you." she grinned back, thinking she'd gladly let Billy lead her anywhere. As they moved to the beat of their own melody, Billy's hands were sliding up and down her back then resting at the top of her butt. She had her hands and arms draped over his shoulders, and his movements back and forth became a little deeper as his hips rocked into hers in sensual, circular movements. Together, their dance became one fluid wave of motion. She felt his hands move up and as he reached the bottom of her shirt, he grabbed onto either side and still moving her back and forth, he pulled her shirt up over her head, letting it fall to the floor, one hand grabbing her ass. Their bodies moved closer to grinding with each of their steps forward and backward. He kept moving her with his body, Maggie's hands sliding down and holding his hips as he pulled his own shirt over his head and let that fall to the floor too, then grabbed onto her ass again and pulled her close. She could feel their hearts pounding together. The rhythmic thumping becoming the beat to their song, steady and deep. She slid her hands up his back, into his hair, and down his neck, softly gazing up at him. Then opened palmed, she ran her hands over his chest, kissing him gently, her mouth open and her bottom lip dragging along as she kissed him. Smelling his skin, soaking in the warmth of his body. He pulled her up closer against himself, now grinding into her harder. His mouth finding hers, opening slightly, pressed together softly, their tongues just touching and still they danced. Maggie trailed her fingers down his chest, down his stomach, down to his pants and undid them, pulling them open. He pulled her in closer, holding his leg between her legs and rubbing her against him. She slid her hands down the back of his pants and grabbed and squeezed his ass, pressing her chest against his. Gently sliding his hands across her body, Billy found his way to her pants and undid them, sliding one hand down the back and squeezing her ass and holding onto it firmly, still moving to the rhythm of their heart beats. His hands were sliding back up and undoing her bra, and he leaned down to kiss her shoulders. He slid each strap off and pulled her bra right down off her arms. She felt it land on the floor, as his hands slid up on either side of her neck, stopping at the base of her head, then leaning down and with soft, pleasant moans, kissed long and deep, moving their bodies together slowly. Billy offered his thigh for her to grind, Maggie back to squeezing his ass as she pressed against him. Then Billy was sliding his body down hers, licking her breasts on the way, pulling her pants and underwear down, he kissed her stomach. Then making his way back up, he pulled his pants and underwear down and came back up to kiss her mouth again. Now naked and still dancing together, they ran their hands all over the back of each other's bodies. He slid himself, hard and very erect, straight between her legs, and she was wet enough for him to glide between, back and forth, moving close, along her center while they caressed and kissed one another. Billy took Maggie's body in his hands, and turned her around so her back was against him, and he slid himself between her legs again, their hips rocking together. His hands sliding along the outside of her body, he held her hips, then he ran his hands up and across her stomach, over her breasts, pinching and squeezing, one hand running across her chest to hold and squeeze the opposite breast, the other hand sliding back down and rubbing his fingers between her legs, still gliding from behind. Maggie stretched her arms up around his neck, her head against his chest, her chin slightly raised, breathing heavily. She pulled his face down to meet hers and they were just able to reach out their tongues and lick playfully. Then, Billy spun her back around, picking her up as he moved them toward the bed. He laid down and pulled her on top. Moving their bodies right up onto the bed, hands rubbing everywhere. He held her hair back from her face, cradling her head with his hands, looking up at her and kissing, one short kiss after another, both gazing deeply into each other's eyes. And all at once she was kissing him so hard, holding his hands down on the bed and running her body back and forth over him.

"Maggie... I want... to taste you," he said between kisses. She kissed harder still. Then suddenly, Billy was flipping her over and leaning over top of her. Her heart raced at the suddenness and she tried to pull him down to enter, but it was Billy's turn to finish the game they'd started earlier. Now he grabbed her hands and held them down on the bed, their fingers linked and grasping. He was running his face along hers, down to her neck where he sucked softly, and ran his tongue down to her nipples, flicking them, sucking them, then back up to her neck. He let go of her hands, and curled his body down, kissing her breasts and he moved farther down her body, kissing all the way down into the soft hair above her center. Breathing deeply, her body rising and aching for him as he proceeded to run his tongue over her clit, then over her thigh, between her legs and over the other thigh. Reaching up and pulling gently on her nipples as his tongue made its way back between her legs, giving her a few warm, wide, deep, wet licks, moaning his hunger for her as he kissed and softly sucked her warm center. Maggie was squirming as he moved back up her body.

"God Billy, take me!" she moaned. He held her body and flipped her over, face first on the bed, laying down on top of her. Then on all fours, he reached out and gently moved her hair to one side. Billy leaned down, and licked her mouth, then kissed her neck, and proceeded to run his tongue down her spine, as he held her hips. She felt him get up and run his hands down to her ass, squeezing firmly before grabbing onto the tops of her legs, and spreading them open. She felt his fingers sliding along her, fondling and pressing into her as he kissed the small of her back, his body moving back up along hers, then pushing himself inside her as he laid on top of her again, one of his hands slipping under her body and rubbing her clit, massaging with a constant pulsing pressure as he slid himself in and out. It was a completely different and delicious sensation for Maggie, and she was so aroused that she had orgasm after orgasm.

"Mmm, Billy. Ohh my God." She felt like she might scream. The way he played her body was pure magic.

He groaned and growled with pleasure at her arousal, gliding slowly, making her wetter and wetter. Billy flipped her onto her back again, and as he was gliding deeply, in and out, Maggie called out his name, no longer able to hold back, crying out with delight.

"Billy!" Her eyes were rolling as she exploded with ecstasy.

"Mag, you feel soo good," he said. She felt him getting closer, and bending her legs up and sliding in harder and faster he moaned a loud "Awww." The sound breathily escaped his mouth as he finished with his hips gyrating and then gently landing on top of her again.

"Billy, that was unbelievable!" she panted in his ear.

Cuddling up snuggly against her, his face near her ear, through his own heavy pants he said,

"You are unbelievably hot!" She kissed his face and hugged him tight. "You make me so crazy Mag!" he added and lifted his head to kiss her again.

"Mmm, we make beautiful music together," Maggie purred, her eyes warm and dreamy as she looked into his crinkled smiling soulful stare. Like their very first night together, they laid there holding on and touching each other all night. And like that first night, they attacked each other again before falling asleep with smiles on their faces.

CHAPTER 12

When Maggie awoke, Billy was still sleeping. Their bodies spooned together, his body pressed up against her back with his arm over her, she pulled him in closer and wriggled her body up against him cozily. With her eyes still closed, she took a deeply contented breath and smiled to herself, the lingering effects of the night's activities still deliciously dancing, fresh and sweet in her mind. Then the realization of their night hitting her like a mac truck. *That was our last night,* she thought to herself, suddenly overcome with a bottomless sense of anxious sadness. Everything turning in towards her, dark and heavy and gut wrenching. She pulled herself against Billy as tightly as she possibly could, running her hand along his arm, holding his hand near her face, and kissing him.

"Mmmm, Morning Mag," came his sexy raspy voice, sleepily from behind her, his face nuzzling into her hair and hugging her tight.

"Morning Lover," she managed, hiding the pain in her voice as best she could. She heard him inhale deeply as he nuzzled his face into her hair a little further and rested his cheek against her neck.

"Mmm, I like the sound of that," he growled hungrily.

She felt her neck tingle with electricity at his warm breath. They stayed like that, Billy holding her tight for a time, then he started to kiss her neck, and run his hand up and down her arm. The desire between them was infectious and insatiable. With each caress, their breathing quickened, with each snuggle closer, the energy between them building, until he was softly sweeping his hand over the front of her body. Maggie reached back and ran her hand over his hip and down the top of his leg. As she felt Billy, hard against her body, she pressed her bottom against him and his hand moved down to her hip, pulling her more snuggly against his body. Their hips moving together, Maggie pressing against him, Billy pushing himself along the crease between her legs, his hand holding her breast as he kissed her neck. Maggie turned over to face him, her arms and legs wrapping around him so tightly. Billy pulled her so close, their mouths pressed right up together, hardly moving, as he held her leg over his hip and entered her. It was so impassioned and yet still so tender. His lips on her skin were like fire, her heart aching and soaring at the same time. His hands holding her face, her fingers running through his hair, their oneness felt so forever to them, and yet so like a dream that was fading away with each fleeting attempt to hold onto it. They moved slowly, so lovingly. It was just so beautifully deep, and yet, somehow so sad.

"Billy," Maggie whispered as they rocked their bodies in waves of delight. "I love you." His hands gently grasped her hair, kissing her with slow, deep, methodical movements, and as he moved in and out of her body, he looked into her eyes and said,

"I love you, Maggie." Pulling each other in deeply again, the climax exquisite but somehow raw, unfinished, even as they shuddered together. As they fell against each other, holding on tightly, their bodies quivering deliciously, slowly, then relaxing, Maggie felt tears running from her eyes. Billy had reached up to hold her face in his strong tender hands, and rubbed his nose on hers, kissing her lips softly, he looked into her eyes, wiping the tears away and kissed her again.

"Oh Mag," he said, and she nestled down into his safe warm embrace, breathing him in as she rested against his chest, and Maggie thought to herself, in a bittersweet haze, *so that's what it means to make love.*

They laid together, not talking, every so often hugging a little tighter, kissing each other's faces, necks, chests and arms all over, running their hands through each other's hair, then just gazing, lost in each other's eyes. Billy breathed her in deeply.

"Mmm, I'll never forget your smell." His words were low and husky. Maggie snuggled in, curling herself around him, and he wrapped her up tightly in his strong embrace. Holding onto their last, complete heart and soul-bared tenderness with one another. Their young naked bodies, so truthful, blissful, sweet; loving moments, they soaked them all up, right down to the very last second they still had together.

When they finally let go, they gathered up their things, sitting right next to each other on the side of the bed as they dressed. Leaning shoulder to shoulder, looking into one another's eyes with such sadness.

"We better go Mag," Billy said, his voice almost a whisper, cracking slightly. He stood up and reached down to hold her hands and pulled her up against him. Maggie looked up and smiled at him as he held her face again and kissed her so very softly and sweetly. She inhaled him and knew she'd never forget the way he smelled either. There was a tug at her heart at the thought of it being all but a memory soon. They didn't giggle climbing the balcony and sneaking through Sam and Chris's room. And as they went their separate ways on the landing, it wasn't with big smiles and floating hearts.

"Hiya Maggie," Tina said as she went into their room. Maggie lifted her hand slightly to wave but didn't say anything. She noticed Tina looking across at Bridget.

"Hey, you doing alright?" asked Bridget. Maggie climbed up onto her bunk and without even thinking, started to pack up her sleeping bag and pillow. She felt like she was moving in slow motion through someone else's dream. The other two had already finished packing and were taking their things out to the landing.

"Maggie, do you want some help packing up?" came Tina's sweet, concerned voice. Maggie shook her head and gave her friends a slight smile.

"No…thanks," she replied. The girls left the room, closing the door behind them. Maggie sat on the bunk staring out the sliding glass door for ages. Not really feeling or thinking, just staring. She heard Jon and Sam carrying on outside the door, laughing and yelling and that seemed to shake her out of her numbness slightly and bring her back to the job at hand. Most of her things were at the end of her bunk still. She hadn't really spent much time in there, so there wasn't much to gather up. Climbing down, she walked around the room, gathering up anything else she found. The door opened, it was Bridget and Tina.

"Maggie, we're leaving in about an hour and a half, are you sure you don't want some help?" Bridget asked, walking over to her. Maggie shook her head again.

"No, really, I'm fine," she lied. Tina suddenly wrapped her arms around Maggie and hugged her. Maggie appreciated it and held her friend's arm resting her head against her.

"Thanks Tina," she said as Tina stepped back and smiled at her. "I'll be fine though. I'll meet you downstairs in a few minutes." Hesitating for a moment before leaving the room, Bridget and Tina left her again.

Maggie put the last of her things into her suitcase and zipped it up. She reached up to her bunk and grabbed the sweater she'd borrowed from Billy, and pulled it over her head, smelling it and smiling as she hugged it. *Mmmm* she thought *smells like Billy*. Then she walked over to the sliding door and looked out at the mountains. A gentle smile crept across her face, and she closed her eyes, inhaling deeply. The passion, and excitement, and fun she'd had with Billy, forever engraved on her heart. Sweet and delicious. She'd carry those thoughts and feelings within her, with affectionate fondness, forever. The week had gone by so quickly and yet somehow it had felt like a whole lifetime. She was different. Nothing like the Maggie Ashberry who had first walked through the doors of The Cabin. She turned, grabbed her backpack, and slid her arms through the straps, picked up her suitcase and walked out of her room onto the landing. People were coming in and out of the rooms, busily, walking up and down the stairs, carrying luggage, laughing, hugging, the odd kiss here and there. Maggie walked down in a trance, feeling as if she was walking through a parallel dimension from the others, almost feeling like she had left her body, as she drifted along slower than the seemingly sped up movement of her friends, as if they were rushing past her as she tried to wade through thick sand. She sat her things down by the open door and suddenly had the urge to scream out, "NOOO! I DON'T WANT TO GO!"

Maggie stood looking out at the sun's progress over the mountains. People walked in and out to put their bags out on the front porch, but they seemed muted somehow. She knew every sunrise and sunset would remind her of Billy and she felt a complete feeling of despair as she watched the light stretching across the snow.

The cab for Maggie, Bridget, Tina, Sam, and Chris would

be arriving around eleven. Knowing she only had about an hour left was almost too overwhelming for Maggie, and just as she was deciding the Earth could swallow her up any second now, that she'd rather that fate then to be without her Billy, she felt his hands on her arms from behind her, running gently up and down, then wrapping around her, hugging her close. Billy snuggled his face down on her shoulder and against her face.

"You okay Mag?" he asked softly. She didn't answer but tried to give a little nod. He squeezed her a little tighter.

"Feel like going for a walk?" he asked, and she turned around in his arms and hugged him. She didn't feel like moving. He held her tight.

"Mag?" he said, and she finally looked up at him. He smiled at her, and she smiled back, neither one of them doing a very good job at pretending their hearts weren't breaking.

Becky and Justin were over on the couch, and called out to them when they noticed the two of them standing there.

"Hey, you two, want to join us?" Becky asked. Billy smiled at them but shook his head.

"Thanks guys, but we're going to go for a walk." Becky looked at Maggie, knowing how much the two of them would miss each other.

"Oh, cool, we'll join you!" said Justin happily, but Becky grabbed his arm and shook her head at him. He looked clueless for a moment, but Becky smiled at Billy, and he and Maggie grabbed their jackets and pulled on their boots, stepping out into the bright sunshine. They walked hand in hand towards the path at the back, but stopped just before going down, under the canopy of trees. Billy held her arms, giving them a squeeze, smiling his cheeky grin at her, his eyes still twinkling, but a sadness hiding behind the usual cheeky twinkle. She stretched up and he leaned down, her hands on his arms as his hands rose up to cradle her face, their lips meeting with such hunger, pressing into one another deeply, almost desperately. They walked a little way down the path, arms wrapped around each other, Maggie's head resting against his body, his head on hers. When they got to the sign that pointed to the hot springs or into town, they turned around and headed back.

"Let's just run away Mag!" he said, half-jokingly, half expectantly. She grinned.

"Wouldn't that be wonderful Billy," she answered. They stopped a few more times on their way back to stare at each other and kiss as many times as they could.

When they went back into the cabin, Adam and Kim were saying goodbye to everyone. Billy and Maggie hugged them and wished them safe travels, as their cabby loaded up their things, then they climbed into the back seat together. They watched as they drove away, everyone waving.

"God Billy, I don't think I can do this," Maggie suddenly said to him as they stood waving. He took her hand in his and looked deeply into her eyes.

"I know Mag." He looked close to tears too, which just

made the ones she was holding back start flowing. The two of them kissed through tears. Billy wiped them away as fast as they were falling from her emerald, green eyes. "Come on Mag, how about we go say goodbye to everyone, it's almost eleven." and he pulled her along, back into the cabin. The others were scattered about, some still gathering up their things, a few more people saying their goodbyes. Becky and Justin came over and Becky pulled Maggie in for a big hug.

"It was amazing meeting you Maggie. You take care of yourself now." Maggie gave her a big squeeze back.

"You too Becky. You'll take care of him for me, right?" Becky nodded, and they smiled at each other as they pulled apart. Justin turned and hugged Maggie.

"All the best to you Maggie!" he said, she smiled at him and nodded.

"Yep, you too Justin! Good luck with your plans on moving into the mountains." He smiled broadly at her. She hugged Jon and Gwen, and Tammy, then looking around for Cindy and Adam, everyone laughed.

"One last romp before leaving?" Chris said coming up behind them.

"Happy trails dude's and dudettes!" said Jon, waving at Maggie's group heading out the door.

As they stepped out, a cab pulled up, and Maggie's heart sank, waiting to see who it was for. Then as the friends stood on the front porch together, they heard the cabby call out.

"Sam?" The driver got out of the car as he called out to

the group on the porch. Maggie turned around and looked up at Billy. He picked up her things and took them over to the car, then came back over to her and pulled her to the side.

"I'll never forget you, Maggie." He wrapped his arms around her and picked her up, giving her a long, lingering kiss, then letting her slide down to stand, he held her face and added, "And I do love you. I didn't know it was possible to love someone instantly. You've shown me a love I didn't know existed." She held his hands and kissed him back.

"I'll miss you so much Billy. I don't know what I'm going to do without you." She was crying again and his eyes were welling up too.

"Don't cry Mag." and he kissed her forehead. "Oh Maggie, please don't cry." He kissed her whole face, his fingers softly squeezing her curls as he held back his own tears.

"I love you, Billy." And with one last kiss, their hands holding tight, she stepped away from him, turning back to look at him. He pulled her back and wrapping their arms around each other completely, holding tight, they kissed like the world was about to end. Pulling one another in, feeling so much love and adoration for each other, understanding what they had was special and hating the unfairness of their parting. Then with their faces resting together, tears running down their cheeks, they smiled softly at each other. They couldn't let go. They held on as tight as they could. Their bodies painfully trying to ignore their emanant separation.

"I'll love you forever, Billy," Maggie whispered, sobbing softly.

"I'll never stop loving you Mag," he whispered back. The cabby gave a little honk of his horn and holding hands, the young lovers kissed one last time. Maggie pulled herself away, her hand trailing behind her, still in Billy's, feeling his fingers slipping away, letting go, until she was walking alone, sobbing. Her heart, aching. Then, trying to pull herself together, holding in tears, she climbed into the cab. Maggie closed the door and rolled down the window, looking at Billy one last time, memorizing any beautiful detail she might have missed about him. He looked so sad watching her go. Then, just as the cab started to pull away, Billy called out.

"Maggie!" He yelled, and she felt her heart soar for a moment as she looked back and saw him running towards her. The cab stopped and Billy opened Maggie's door. He leaned down and held her face, kissing her pressingly. Maggie held his wrists, wishing more than anything they could stay in each other's arms.

"We need to go Maggie." Bridget's voice seemed distant and Maggie realized she had been holding her breath, inhaling suddenly as she was pulled back out of her world with Billy. Kissing softly, then looking deeply into one another's souls one the last time. Billy's beautiful blue eyes were full of tears as he backed away and closed the door. She couldn't breathe. How would she ever breathe without her Billy? The cab started moving again, and they slowly made their way down the driveway. The radio was on, quietly. She couldn't make out what the DJ was saying but as she turned and looked out the back window at Billy standing there, "I Will Never Be The Same" started playing and she felt her heart shatter completely and painfully in that very moment. She felt like her whole body was breaking. How would she live without him? The pain was too much.

No one said anything to her the whole ride to the airport. Maggie heard her friends talking but didn't really know what they were saying. She felt like she was at the end of a very long tunnel, their voices seemed distant and muffled. Maggie was physically aching. Her heart was painfully breaking. Her stomach knotted in agony. It took everything in her to just keep breathing. Boarding the plane in a fog, she took the window seat and sat absentmindedly staring out of it the whole flight home. As they grabbed their luggage and went out to the passenger pick up to find Bridget's dad, Maggie saw Pete walking towards her.

"Maggie!" he yelled as he came up to hug her. She hugged him back, at first reluctantly, but the familiarity was some-how comforting, and although her heart was breaking for an-other, she was glad to have his arms holding her now. On the ride home, Pete went on about how the week had dragged on, waiting to see her, seemingly oblivious to the sadness en-gulfing her. He said he hoped she hadn't gotten into too much trouble, laughing to himself, and that her parents were going to be glad she was home again.

Bridget's dad dropped Maggie off, and she grabbed her things, thanking him. It was very late, so Pete said he'd come by the next day. Maggie waved to her friends, turned towards the farmhouse, and walked into a cheerful welcome from her family. Going through the motions, numbly answering any questions about what fun she had at the cabin, leaving out 90 percent of what she had got up to. She told them all about how beautiful it was and how she'd learned how to ski, kind of, and how amazing the hot spring pool was and a little about the people she'd met too.

When she finally excused herself to go up to bed, her mother followed her, helping her with her luggage.

"It's lovely to have you home Margaret. I've missed having my girl around," her mom told her as she put her arm around Maggie's shoulder and gave her a hug.

"Good to see you too mom," Maggie replied with a small smile.

"Is everything okay Margaret?" Her mom asked, looking at her with concern. Maggie nodded and forced a smile, trying not to cry, before taking her things into her room. Her mom stayed near the doorway, her head tilting to one side.

"Margaret?" she said questioningly. "Did something happen dear?" She asked. Turning to face her mom, Maggie sat on the edge of her bed and shook her head again.

"No mom, nothing happened. Just tired." She smiled at her mom again. Her mom stared at her for a moment, reading her and knowing Maggie was keeping something from her.

"Really mom, everything's fine," Maggie added and her mom nodded and turned to leave.

"Okay Margaret, but if you need to talk about anything…" She turned back and gave Maggie a mom look, her eyes smiling kindly at her daughter.

"Yep, thanks mom. Goodnight," Maggie replied as her mom closed her door. As soon as she heard her mom's footsteps on the stairs she fell over onto her pillow. No longer able to hold back tears, Maggie sobbed quietly. Her heart hurt and she wasn't sure how she'd go on.

CHAPTER 13

Maggie was soon right back to her old duties. Her world didn't seem to hold the same wonder as it used to though. Nothing was as beautiful as it was before she met Billy. Nothing tasted as good or smelled as sweet. She now just existed, wondering when reality would set in again. The days all blended together in a haze. And as the days turned to weeks, then months, Maggie soon found herself a year into nursing school. Traveling back and forth from the college to the farm, she found that time seemed to move faster and faster. Robotically working on the farm, day after day, and studying late into the night, Maggie felt like she needed a break and some joy. She started volunteering a few hours a week at the local doctor's office, and still often found herself daydreaming about Billy and what might have been. Her thoughts always ended with their heartbreaking goodbye. She kept suppressing her thoughts of her week and the true love and the passion they had shared. Trying to swallow the pain of leaving him and pushing her feelings down in order to numb her broken heart. Instead, she trudged along, impassively, being the girl, everyone wanted her to be. Good *old* Maggie.

After completing her second year of school and having

finally given Pete a solid yes to his proposal, plans for their wedding were well under way. Maggie got better at pushing Billy out of her mind and put her thoughts into her studies and her future with Pete. Eventually, the fog lifted slightly, and she found some joy in things again. Things never felt quite right though. It was like somehow everything she was hoping for existed just beyond a veil. She could never quite find where to pull it back, so she could step into her true existence, but always felt like it was lingering somewhere at the end of her fingertips. She was a new Maggie but stuck in the old Maggie's life. And yet, life just kept on.

Maggie would be moving into the Baker's farmhouse with Pete and his father after the wedding. His dad was on a waitlist for the county senior's residence and would soon be moving. Maggie didn't mind Pete's father, for visits, but she was relieved she wouldn't be marrying into the responsibility of taking care of her father-in-law right off the get go. She knew she'd become the home nurse and as newlyweds, it wouldn't be ideal. She and Pete had plans to sell his family's farm after his father moved out. Pete had secured a good job at an accountant's office in a nearby town, that paid well and came with benefits. He had never enjoyed being a farm boy, so he was eager to leave that behind and work in a clean, animal-free office for a change. They planned to use the money from the farm sale to buy a little place together and use the rest to pay for his father's residence at the nursing home.

Maggie spent a lot of time with Bridget and Tina. Well,

any spare chance she got. She was feeling apprehensive about marriage, and they were the two people that truly understood why.

"Do you think you should try to contact him, Maggie?" Tina asked timidly and with almost as much sadness in her voice as Maggie felt. Maggie smiled softly and shook her head.

"Where would I start? And besides, we said we knew it was just for the week. We are from very different worlds." Maggie stared off into nowhere. "We agreed." She added softly, absentmindedly holding and fondling the gold chain around her neck. "Just a silly crush. It just wasn't meant to be anything more than that." Her voice trailed off in a whisper. Neither Tina nor Bridget brought Billy up again and turned their efforts instead to planning their best friend's wedding with her.

Maggie soon had her dress picked out and dresses for Tina and Bridget, who were her two bridesmaids. All three dresses were long, with spaghetti straps, and made of silk. Maggie's was white of course, and had a layer of white lace on top. It was light and very summery. Her friends, the same, except Tina in teal and Bridget in purple. It would be a summer wedding at the beginning of August, and the service would take place at the little church in town, followed by the reception at the Ashberry farm. Of course, every relative Maggie had was invited and, being the only daughter, her parents spared nothing for it to be perfect.

With only two years left until graduation, and becoming

a registered nurse, and a wedding just around the corner as well as her regular duties on the farm, Maggie had little time to think about anything else, which was good. She was even starting to feel a little more like her old self again.

Deeply occupied with wedding plans and late nights studying, Maggie was still very busy helping run the farm, and she soon became a robot version of herself, pushing through the pain that still surfaced if she let her guard down. Although she had a lot on her plate, she was up before the sun every day, taking care of things on the farm, before heading off to school, and managed to do it all with her big Maggie smile.

* * *

"Margaret! Margaret!" but as she raked up the hay for the horses, listening to her new Melissa Ethridge tape on her walk-man, Maggie didn't hear her mother calling her. "I Will Never Be the Same" was playing and she had it turned right up, singing along. Suddenly, she felt an urgent tap on her shoulder and pulled her headphones down, turning around to see her mom standing with an irritated look on her face.

"Margaret, must you listen to that while you're doing chores!?" Maggie shrugged.

"Sorry Mom. What's up?" Her mother shook her head and gave Maggie a little grin.

"Oh Margaret, you, and your music! Peter's on his way dear, to take us to the rehearsal dinner. Best get yourself cleaned up. Oh Margaret, you are going to make the most beautiful bride!" Her mom smiled then walked back towards the house.

THE END

About the Author

Katherine Waite-Gracie is a single, homeschooling mom of two great kids, two fur babies, and a fish named Mr. Malory. Growing up in a small town in Ontario, loving community and nature, she spent most of her time in the water or taking long walks with friends, daydreaming of a life full of wooded, secluded comforts and spending her days and nights with a partner as loving and as passionate about life as herself. Before writing romance novels, Katherine attained degrees and certificates in Intervention, Reiki, Children's Yoga Instruction, and Animal Specialist Programs. She spends her nights continuing to write and has recently finished the 5th and final book in The Maggie Ashberry Series, as well as working on four other novels.

LinkedIn: www.linkedin.com/in/kat-waite-gracie-3681928a
Facebook:www.facebook.com/kat.waitegracie
Instagram: https://www.instagram.com/katsmyth/

www.ingramcontent.com/pod-product-compliance
Lightning Source LLC
Chambersburg PA
CBHW071330120626
46546CB00002B/513